SOLVING YOUR FINANCIAL PROBLEMS

Getting Out of Debt, Repairing Your Credit and Dealing with Bankruptcy

Richard L. Strohm

Chelsea House Publishers

Philadelphia

First printed in hardback edition in 1997 by Chelsea House Publishers.

1 3 5 7 9 8 6 4 2

Library of Congress Cataloging-in-Publication Data

Strohm, Richard L.
  Layman's law guides. Solving your financial problems / by Richard L. Strohm.
    p. cm.
Rev. ed. of: Solving your financial problems. 2nd ed. c1994.
Includes index.
  ISBN 0-7910-4443-2 (hc)
  1. Bankruptcy—United States—Popular works. 2. Debtor and creditor—United States—
Popular works. I. Solving your financial problems. II. Title.
KF1524.6.S768 1997
346.73'078—dc21   96-49390
                                                               CIP

Table of Contents

I. How to Use This Publication

This publication is designed to help people in financial trouble. Often we hear about how easy it is to avoid paying your bills by "declaring bankruptcy." It is **not** that easy, nor is bankruptcy a cure-all for every situation. **Often bankruptcy is completely unnecessary.** Even if bankruptcy is the best option, its effect on your financial future is serious and long lasting.

> Even if bankruptcy is the best option, the effect on your financial future is serious and long lasting.

This publication explains how you can get help for your financial problems and explore some alternatives to bankruptcy. However, in certain severe cases, bankruptcy may be the only alternative. If you are wondering about what happens when you file for bankruptcy, this publication can answer your questions. It describes how the bankruptcy court works, what happens in court, what kinds of property you are entitled to keep, and what you must give up if you elect to pursue certain bankruptcy options.

Solving Your Financial Problems is designed to inform you of your rights. Often we feel trapped because we do not know what help is available. In order for you to make an informed decision based upon all of the alternatives, you must know your legal rights and responsibilities. Once you have an understanding of your rights and obligations, you then will be in a position to work with a professional in pursuing any option that you choose.

But first, a few words of caution. The law of bankruptcy, like any area of the law, is complicated. Whether or not you may benefit from the protection of the bankruptcy court depends upon your particular and unique circumstances. No two situations are alike. In fact, sometimes cases which appear to be "identical" to most people are **not**. This is why you should never make a decision to take action (or to take no action) based upon what someone else has done or has told you, even though it may appear to you that your situation is the same as another's.

This publication can help you prepare for your first visit with a credit counselor, attorney or other professional.

The information presented here can be used best to gain a solid understanding of your rights and the law. But please remember that the law of bankruptcy and the legal procedure used in bankruptcy courts are very different from any other area of the law. **I urge you to seek legal counsel from a licensed attorney concerning your particular legal situation.** This publication is **not** a substitute for qualified counsel. While the information contained here can help you understand your rights and the law, it does not substitute for a good lawyer. A decision about what is appropriate for you should be made only after talking with a licensed and qualified attorney.

This publication can help you prepare for your first visit with a credit counselor, attorney or other professional. If you know something about the law and your rights, you can make better use of the professional's time. This publication will also give you an understanding of what documents the professional will need in order to help you with your financial problems.

I hope my book will help you make the very best informed decisions in resolving your financial problems **and** save you money in the process. Your financial problems will be easier to face when you know what the law says about your situation—both good and bad. Since a lawyer charges by the hour, the more you understand about what the law requires and how the court operates, the more effective and economical his or her advice to you will be.

> The more you understand about your rights, the more effective and economical a lawyer's advice to you will be.

Congratulations on your purchase. It is your first step on the road back to financial health!

Richard L. Strohm, Esq.
Scottsdale, Arizona
January, 1994

II. Bankruptcy Is Not Your Only Option If You Are in Financial Trouble

The simple answer to the question, "Is bankruptcy for me?" depends on a great many factors. There may be, and usually are, other ways of resolving your financial trouble without resorting to bankruptcy. There is no easy formula or "rule of thumb" about how far into debt you can be before you consider bankruptcy. Each case is different. Even so, you always should think of bankruptcy as a last resort. **For many people in financial trouble, bankruptcy is not only undesirable, it is completely unnecessary**. Let's look at some other options which can help and which you should consider *before* bankruptcy.

First, begin with a budget. Identify the total amount of your monthly expenses. These ought to include all of your usual monthly obligations, as well as spending money, gasoline and car maintenance costs, entertainment expenses, and a cushion for yourself. Be sure to include those expenses which may not be due each month, but still must be paid. For example, quarterly or semi-annual insurance payments should be prorated on a monthly basis and added to your list of expenses.

Next, compute your net monthly income from all sources. Compare expenses and income for the next six months. Include any anticipated changes in expenses or income during this six-month period.

> You always should think of bankruptcy as a last resort.

Finally, look at your expenses and determine what you can cut. Are there any expenses that could be reduced? Deferred? Obviously, if you can bring your expenses within your net income, you are not ready for bankruptcy!

III. Sample Monthly Budget

On page 11 is a sample budget. The left-hand column shows typical expenses, the right shows sample figures used by typical bankruptcy trustees as a guideline in determining what is reasonable. **This is only a guide.**

What if expenses still exceed income? Before seriously considering bankruptcy, be absolutely certain you really have serious and **long lasting** financial problem. In the case of a temporary interruption of income bills, may be unpaid or only partially paid. As a result, creditors may hound or harass you to bring your account current. Bankruptcy is usually unnecessary in this instance as well, particularly if your income will be back to normal within a few months.

Often, the creditors who are pressing you for payments are unaware that you have a problem. Your first job should be to contact each of your creditors and explain truthfully and completely all of the circumstances giving rise to your inability to pay. Then, try to work out a payment schedule with each of them in a fashion which fits your present budget limitations. This is also true in the case where your

Get an accurate picture of your finances; then contact each creditor and explain that you're having difficulty.

problem is not "temporary," but the result of the overuse of credit cards. Before you seriously consider bankruptcy, call all of your creditors and tell them you have a problem and propose to pay them what you **can** afford, until the debt is satisfied.

If a creditor agrees to accept less, put it in writing!

Please keep in mind that a creditor may agree to accept a partial payment, but **can** legally sue for the balance. Make sure the creditor promises **in writing** not to sue if you make only partial payments in accordance with the agreement between you and the creditor.

If you try to work out a new payment plan with your creditors without professional help, be sure not to promise to pay too much. It is better to leave yourself a cushion and a little extra in your new budget for emergencies. It is far better to promise to pay $5 each month and make those payments without failure when due, than to promise to pay $50 each month and not live up to your word.

When discussing your situation with your creditors, ask each to waive, or give up, his right to collect accruing interest charges on the unpaid balance of what you owe. There is **no requirement** that they do this, but they may be willing to suspend interest if they know you are serious about making your payments. They may require you to surrender your credit cards or not draw any more credit if you have another type of credit arrangement.

Also consider asking for a grace period in which no payments would be due. This would give you an opportunity to have some temporary relief while you work out a new budget which will work under your present circumstances. You might also request that the creditor help you create a new budget.

SAMPLE MONTHLY BUDGET:

1. Rent/Home Mortgage Payments (including lot rental for trailers)	Variable, usually 25%-35% of gross income, determined on a case by case basis
2. Utilities	Electricity $250; heat $50; water $30; telephone $50
3. Food	$210 singles; $315 couples; $140 teens
4. Clothing	$30 for each family member
5. Laundry & Cleaning	$10 for each family member; $25 for singles
6. Newspapers, Periodicals, Books, School Books	$20 per family; $20 newspapers
7. Medical & Drug	Determined on a case by case basis, medical insurance is a factor
8. Insurance (not deducted from wages)	Auto: variable, verification required; health & other(renter's, life, etc.) variable, verification required
9. Transportation (gas, oil, tires, etc.)	$150 per vehicle; bus fare per family if no vehicle $50
10. Recreation	$50-$80 (includes cable T.V.)
11. Club & Union Dues (not deducted from wages)	Business or job related ONLY
12. Taxes (not deducted from wages)	Not to exceed normal deductions, if not income related, specify
13. Alimony, Maintenance or Support Payments	Variable, verification required
14. Other Payments (for support of dependents living at home)	Determined on a case by case basis
15. Other (describe)	Church contributions, etc. determined on a case by case basis
16. Home Maintenance	Only if home is owned $50
17. Misc. & Contingency Expenses	Per family $50-$75

11

IV. Slashing and Saving to Stay Afloat

"Nobody wants to be a slave to their money anymore," notes Mary Hunt, editor of *Cheapskate Monthly*. "Even people who aren't worried about getting fired are craving richer but simpler life styles."

You have probably figured out that getting out of debt is your number one ticket to financial stability. Paying off high interest credit card balances helps you lower expenses, and gives you more cash to pay other bills as well as to save.

Pay off your high interest credit card balances.

There are a number of other smart moves that you can make which may result in cutting your budget by 30 percent or more. While some of the suggested options may seem radical, evaluate your particular situation. Do your circumstances require major surgery or simply a quick repair? By investigating the options listed below, you should be able to come up with an overall strategy for improving your financial picture immediately.

Relocation

While this is a drastic remedy, if you or your spouse are one of the more than 400,000 Americans who have lost jobs in the past two years, it may be time for you to look to relocating to a different part of the country. Job prospects are higher and living costs lower in many parts of the west and south than in the northeast and midwest.

Such things as monthly utility bills can be 10 percent to 30 percent below what you are paying now in a more favorable climate. Even such things as junior college tuition and property taxes may drastically drop in less populated states such as Arizona, Utah and Nevada.

Refinancing Your Mortgage
In the past two years, almost 20 percent of all Americans who owed mortgages refinanced their homes. This is because interest rates are at the lowest level since the 1970s. As this book went to press, interest rates were hovering around 7 percent. If you are able to qualify for a refinancing loan, you may be able to cut your monthly payments by 25 percent or more.

> You can refinance your mortgage, but make sure you understand all of the costs involved.

For example, a 30-year fixed mortgage at a 12.5 percent interest rate involves a monthly payment of principal and interest of $1,067.00. If you are able to refinance at a fixed 6.75 percent rate, your payment would drop 25 percent to $797.00 principal and interest. Not only would you realize significant monthly savings, but over the next fifteen years, you would save approximately $70,000.

But be careful. Make sure you understand all of the costs before you agree to refinance your mortgage. There are a number of closing costs—the "origination fee," for example, is a substantial cost which is *in addition to* the disclosed interest rate. Make sure you know exactly what the loan will cost you.

A good rule of thumb on refinancing is to refinance if you can get a rate one percentage point lower than your current mortgage and you plan to stay in your home long enough to amortize the closing costs. This is generally one to two years.

Scrutinize Property Taxes

Vincent Sczapluski, author of the *Homeowner's Property Tax Relief Kit* (McGraw-Hill, $14.95) estimates that approximately half of the homeowners who challenge their property tax assessments by appealing to a local tax authority obtain 10 percent reductions or more. The National Taxpayers Union in Washington, D.C., will send you a helpful 12-page pamphlet entitled *How to Fight Property Taxes*. This booklet carefully spells out what steps you must take in order to contest your property taxes. Simply send $2 to NTU, 713 Maryland Avenue, N.E., Washington, DC 20002.

> Approximately half of the home-owners who challenge their property taxes obtain 10% reductions.

Load Controllers

A load controller conserves electricity by shutting down or reducing power to certain major appliances which use a great deal of energy. For example, a load controller will cycle your water heater off when the rates are at their highest during the day. Some utility companies will install a load controller for you at no cost. If you have to buy one and have it installed yourself, the cost is between $100 and $1,500 depending on the size of your home. Sometimes you may be able to finance the cost of the load controller. The savings on your utility bills should pay the cost of financing the load controller within one or two years. Some families have realized savings of 40 percent through the use of a load controller.

Long Distance Charges

It is very confusing, given the amount of advertising that the major long distance carriers provide on television, in learning what the truth is about savings. Choosing the right long distance carrier and discount plan may cut your monthly telephone bills by 20 percent if you are making at least six long distance calls per month. Since where you call, the number of calls, and when you call are critical to completing this analysis, you need to know the facts. I would recommend that you send $2 and a self-addressed, stamped envelope to: Telecommunications Research and Action Center, P.O. Box 12038, Washington, DC 20005 to receive a comparison of rates for the five biggest carriers. You can save on phone charges by:

> Find ways to cut down on your long distance phone charges.

◊ eliminating long distance calls between 8 a.m. and 5 p.m. weekdays;
◊ dialing yourself; and
◊ using toll-free numbers (Many businesses have toll-free numbers. Dial 1-800-555-1212 for toll-free information).

Major Purchases

Try to buy big ticket items when they are off season. For example, air conditioners are best purchased in the winter, heaters in the summer. Also, stay alert for new store "Grand

Openings" as well as seasonal promotions. Sometimes discounts of 25 percent to 50 percent below retail are offered on many appliances. According to the editors of *Cut Your Bills In Half* (Rodale Press, $24.95), January and June are the best sale months for purchasing freezers, stoves, ovens and refrigerators. While February and September are best for purchasing air conditioners. It is estimated that the potential savings per unit is between $50 and $200.

Batteries
Batteries are extremely expensive. Alkaline batteries are useless once the charge has been used up. Nickel-cadmium rechargeable batteries are some 600 to 800 times more usable than alkaline. While rechargeable batteries are initially more expensive, they are capable of producing savings several hundred times beyond the cost of their additional cost.

Food
You may be able to reduce your food bills by 50 percent if you join a wholesale food service which sells bulk quantities of meats, juices, pasta, fish and other groceries. Such services will help you plan for your family, and often provide delivery service as part of the cost. A typical example of such a service is Colorado Prime (1-800-365-9498) which is one of the biggest in the country. But check your telephone book under "Food Plans."

Similarly, you may be able to join a discount club such as Sam's Club (800-925-6278) or Price

> You may be able to reduce your food bills by purchasing often-used items in bulk.

Club (800-597-7423) which sell groceries, auto supplies, office equipment, cleaning aides, toys, liquor, and other household products. A 1992 study by the Food Marketing Institute found that on average the 700 retail warehouse clubs which exist in the United States typically charge a fee of approximately $25 and offer approximately 26 percent savings over their retail competitors.

It is also possible to grow some of your own vegetables, depending where you live, your climate, and your interest in gardening. You can cut 30 percent from your food budget by using fruits and vegetables you grow yourself. Go the bookstore for a manual on gardening in your area.

> Be creative! Grow your own vegetables and cut 30% from your food budget.

Buying Cars

The Complete Car Cost Guide ($45 plus $4 shipping and handling; 800-227-2665) published by the San José Research Firm, IntelliChoice, is chock full of important tips and cost comparisons on purchasing an automobile. According to IntelliChoice President Peter Levy, "If you are trying to conserve cash, holding onto a well-maintained car may be the smart move." This depends on a number of different factors including the cost of financing and maintenance.

You should choose low-maintenance vehicles. For example, according to *Money Magazine's (March, 1994)* annual car rankings, the five-year maintenance cost for a Ford Aerostar XLT three-door minivan was nearly $2,000 less than that for the lowest-priced Toyota minivan. Considering other expenses such as fuel, insurance, depreciation, financing, and taxes, the difference in ownership costs over five years may be significant. Use this guide as a way of helping you decide which car to purchase.

As in the case of appliances, car dealers offer deep discounts depending on the season. Ron and Melanie Moore in their book *Smart Sense* (Price, Stern & Sloan, $6.98) suggest you may negotiate a reduction in sticker price of 10 percent or more by shopping at the end of the month when dealers are eager to close deals.

Auto Insurance

Save on auto insurance by increasing your collision insurance deductibles from $200 to $500 (providing you can afford to pay the $500 in the event that you are involved in an accident) in order to lower your total auto insurance premium by more than 10 percent. Compare your healthcare coverage with the personal injury protection clause of your auto policy. If you are paying twice for the same benefit, you should consider dropping the personal injury coverage, which may save 15 percent on your total premium. For more information, get Barbara Taylor's book *How to Get Your Money's Worth In Home and Auto Insurance* (McGraw-Hill, $9.95).

Lower your total auto insurance premium by increasing your collision deductible.

Clothing

Clothing is hugely inflated. Veteran off-price dealers such as Marshall's and Loehmann's offer brand-name clothing for 20 percent to 60 percent less than premium retail or department stores. There are approximately 8,000 manufacture-owned outlets across the country that often sell at 50 percent off. Examples include Calvin Klein and Liz Claybourne. If you are interested in shopping in an outlet, pick up *Outlet Shopper's Guide* (Lazar Media Group, $9.95) which provides store hours, selection and directions for 300 outlet centers in all 50 states.

Another way to reduce your spending on clothing, particularly your children's, is to subscribe to newsletters such as *Kid News* ($24.95; P.O. Box 797, Forest Hills, New York 11375), a bi-monthly publication informing parents on where and how to buy designer clothing for kids at up to 85 percent off.

> Shop for clothes at a discount outlet rather than a premium retail or department store.

Another helpful newsletter is *Kids Report* ($29; 212-679-5400) which provides a listing of outlet and showroom sales as well as mail order firms.

Finally, read labels. When possible, buy washable clothes rather than those that require dry cleaning. This is especially important since dry cleaning costs can double and even triple the purchase price of clothing. For example, a pair of $85 wool slacks may require $80 worth of cleaning for a year's wear, assuming 20 dry cleaning trips.

Health Insurance

As this book goes to press, the healthcare controversy looms. For many families, medical care expenses can be devastating. With doctor and hospital bills rising approximately 50 percent faster than the rate of inflation, medical costs and the effect on your budget will be critical in the coming years.

One way to reduce costs is to consider joining an HMO (Health Maintenance Organization). For a flat fee, an HMO will provide quality medical treatment for each member of your family. You pay a nominal amount, usually $5, for office visits and other out-patient treatment services. Prescriptions similarly are provided at a reduced cost, usually for only $2.

For an average family of four with no serious health problem, savings can amount to nearly $1,000 per year.

Healthcare costs vary greatly. Research available programs to see which fits your needs best.

Also be aware that your local government provides free or low-cost services, depending on your income. Contact your county or state health department in the blue pages of the telephone directory for complete information on programs and eligibility requirements. At a minimum, you will need to present some evidence of your financial situation and appear for medical examinations and inoculations at their scheduled times.

Similarly, state medical schools operate community clinics which offer treatment on a fee basis geared toward your income. The care is usually excellent, though there may be much red tape and a great deal of waiting.

If your medical condition is unusual or of particular interest to a staff medical doctor or trainee, you may obtain highly-skilled care for little or no money.

The cost of prescriptions varies depending on whether you choose to purchase a generic or unbranded drug. Generics are the same as branded drugs, in terms of their chemical composition, but because they do not carry a brand name, they are cheaper. Drug manufacturers contend that generic drugs are not the equivalent of brand-name products, but the Food and Drug Administration, Consumers Union and other public interest groups that have studied the situation disagree. Ask your doctor to prescribe generic prescriptions when possible. If you are uncertain whether the drug that has been prescribed for you has a generic equivalent, ask your pharmacist or refer to the *Physicians' Desk Reference*, available at your local bookstore or public library.

> Look for a credit card that charges less than 15% interest on unpaid balances. They're out there!

Credit Cards

A recent survey of credit card rates showed that a great number of issuers of credit cards are charging less than 15 percent interest on unpaid balances. As the economy changes, those institutions charging 18 percent or more are losing a substantial portion of their business. By contrast, cards which carry rates under 15 percent are picking up business. The sustained low interest rates have also contributed to the campaign by credit card issuers to offer consumers lower interest rates for charging. Many

21

consumers are switching over to issuers that offer lower rates.

There are a number of issuers which offer substantially reduced rates, some with and some without annual fees. To get a list of low-cost local, regional and national card issuers, send $5 to CardTrak Research, P.O. Box 1700, Frederick, Maryland 21702.

Utility Bills

In cold climates and in those states where the desert creates as much demand for utility use as cold climates, heating and cooling may account for 60 percent of the total energy you use. Some homes are built with little or no serious insulation. By doubling the thickness of the insulation on your attic floor, for example, you may be able to cut 40 percent of the heat seeping up through the ceilings, or prevent (if you live in a desert climate) 40 percent of the heat trapped in the attic from coming into your living area.

> Check on the insulation in your home. A good system can save you money!

Similarly, windows can contribute to as much as 40 percent of the energy loss in a home. In cold climates, storm windows are good insulation. In warmer climates, double pane or sun reflector film is a good investment. A good rule of thumb is not to invest in any additional changes unless you plan to be in the house long enough to recoup your investment. Other ways to save on your utilities are:

◊ do not run the washing machine or dryer until you have enough for a full load;

◊ in cold climates set your thermostat at 68° during the day and 55° at night;

◊ in warm climates set your thermostat at 80° during the day and 78° at night;

◊ look for air conditioning units with energy efficiency ratios of seven. Instead of using air conditioning, use ceiling fans or smaller mobile fans in order to save kilowatt hours;

◊ use fluorescent lights in garage areas, work areas, kitchens and bathrooms since fluorescent tubes provide approximately 40 percent energy savings over incandescent bulbs.

Life Insurance

"Term" life insurance provides only a specified death benefit. It is less expensive than other types of life insurance products because it does not offer any investment feature.

> What type of life insurance is best for you? Here are some options to consider...

"Whole" life insurance is expensive, but it allows you to build up "cash values" from which you can build an investment base.

Term insurance usually provides coverage in increments of five to seven years. At the end of this period you must then renew and requalify. Usually rates increase upon renewal unless you purchase a term policy with a "level premium."

You may also wish to consider whether a whole life policy, if you have one already, is worth keeping. Whole life is in essence a forced savings plan. If you are able to save on your own, term insurance is a much better value.

Saving On College Tuition

College tuition, even for state-sponsored schools, is rising geometrically. At some private schools it is not unusual to expect costs and fees over a four-year undergraduate period to run as high as $100,000. Even at state-sponsored schools for in-state residents the costs and fees can easily reach $25,000 for four years. There are two ways to fund a college education apart from paying out of pocket:

◊ obtaining a loan; and
◊ obtaining financial aid.

> Costs for a college education can run high...see if you can find a way to obtain financial aid.

The United States Government provides a number of grants, loans and employment programs. There are six types of aid available through the federal government:

◊ college work study programs;
◊ Stafford loans (formerly known as guaranteed student loans);
◊ Perkins loans (5 percent loans through the college financial aid office);
◊ plus loans (low interest loans through a participating lender);
◊ Pell grants (based on need, these awards do not need to be repaid); and
◊ opportunity grants (available through the college, these do not have to be repaid).

In addition to these grants, your state may offer a number of opportunities that you should investigate. For example, some states offer teaching scholarships in which the student is given a stipend if he or she pledges to teach there for a certain period of time after graduation.

Available scholarships are too numerous to mention in this space. It should be noted that a surprising number of scholarships are never used. Some scholarships are awarded on the basis of accomplishment and academics, sports or the arts, and others are based on need. Some special scholarships are also set aside for children of alumni, minorities, etc.

In order to learn more about these programs, contact your local high school guidance counselor or write: Octameron Associates, P.O. Box 3437, Alexandria, VA 22302.

> Remember: Cutting expenses is as effective as earning more money.

Let's assume that some of these, or perhaps all of these options, require too much work for you. If this is the case, you had best reevaluate your commitment to solving your financial problems. At the very least, you should be honest with yourself about whether you are willing to make choices and stick with them in order to realize the overall benefits that will come to you. Remember, there are only two ways to insure your financial success: 1) earning money; 2) keeping it. Cutting expenses is as effective as earning more money, and since it does not involve the same negative tax consequences that earning more money does, it is the easiest route for you to take to insure financial success.

In addition to *The Wall Street Journal* and *Consumer Reports*, I recommend these very good, although obscure, periodicals relating to saving money and slashing expenses:

◊ *The Banker's Secret Bulletin*: quarterly; $19.95/year; typical cover stories: Making a Will, Planning your estate and Avoiding Probate; 914-758-1400.

◊ *Cheapskate Monthly*: monthly; $12.95/year; typical cover story: How to Avoid Debt; 310-630-8845.

◊ *Downscaling*: monthly; $12/year; typical cover story: Back-to School Expenses; 219-566-2488.

◊ *Living Cheap News*: 10 issues; $12/year; typical cover story: Social Security Eligibility; 408-257-1680.

◊ *The Penny Pincher*: six issues; $12/year; typical cover story; How to Save Money Using an Automatic Bread Maker; 516-724-1868.

◊ *Penny Pincher Times*: monthly, $14; typical story: Shopping Thrift Stores for Clothes; Staying in Hostels for Vacations; 407-659-3288.

◊ *The Tightwad Gazette*: monthly; $12/year; typical story: How Being Thrifty Can Make You More Money Than Investing In The Stock Market; 207-524-7962.

V. Asset Protection Techniques That Really Work

Obviously it is important to protect your assets from current or potential claims of creditors. Insurance has been the tried and true method of protecting assets but since coverage limitations now may be inadequate and punitive damages are customarily excluded by the insurer, having insurance is not as safe as it once was.

Similarly, business owners who have personally guaranteed loans or who are in a particularly risky business, and others for whom divorce could result in financial disaster, have the need to maneuver property out of the reach of creditors.

> Make sure you use a lawyer's expertise when executing methods for asset protection.

There are a number of legal methods available to shield many types of assets, however, it is critical to obtain qualified legal counsel on each one of these suggestions. All of them are effective when done properly, but all of them are governed by complicated state laws and federal considerations which must be interpreted by a highly skilled lawyer if they are to be successful. While each of the techniques discussed, if done properly with a lawyer's help, can protect assets, it is important to note that these techniques usually entail losing control over the asset.

Clients often ask me "Why can't all of the assets be given away?" The reason is that most states have adopted some form of fraudulent conveyance law. A fraudulent conveyance statute prohibits simply giving property away to others to avoid a creditor obtaining it. The statutes of the various states are different, but generally they allow creditors to reach any assets which have been transferred with the intent to delay, defraud or hinder creditors. There does not have to be a showing of actual fraud. In other words, the mere fact that the property has been given away (not sold for valuable consideration) is evidence of an intent if:

> A fraudulent conveyance statute prohibits giving property away just to avoid a creditor obtaining it.

◊ by giving the property away the debtor becomes insolvent after the transfer;
◊ the transfer occurs shortly before or after assuming a large debt;
◊ the debtor transfers nearly all of his assets;
◊ the transfer is concealed; or
◊ the transfer is made to the debtor's relatives, close friends or others under his control.

The following techniques are suggested as possible ways of protecting assets which do not run afoul of the rules set forth in the Standard Fraudulent Conveyance Act.

1. A Real Transfer.
Legitimate tax and estate planning asset transfers are protected. You may sell property or give property away to other people where there is a just cause for doing so. It is very important that you document the legitimate reasons for your asset transfer. It is also important to do any transfer well before a creditor makes any claim.

Last-minute attempts to hide or transfer assets can often be rescinded.

2. Spouse Gifts.
While a debtor cannot put everything in his spouse's name in order to avoid creditors, transfers between spouses can provide some protection when there are other legitimate reasons for the transfer. The key to making this option work is to be sure that the transferring spouse gives up all control over and enjoyment of the asset. If you live in a community property state where all of the property of the couple is considered marital property and each enjoys an undivided one-half interest in it, such a transfer usually must be accompanied by a partition agreement.

> Transfers between spouses provides some protection when there are legitimate reasons for the transfer.

3. Family Partnerships.
A limited partnership among family members offers a number of tax and estate planning benefits. Additionally, it can keep the creditors of one partner away from the other partners' shares (although this does not apply to creditors of the partnership itself). The key is establishing a legitimate business and/or tax-planning purpose for the trust.

4. Incorporation.
If your accountant and you decide that a corporation is in your best interest, incorporation provides a great deal of asset protection while permitting continued control of the business by the incorporators. The corporate shield is established between the owners of the business

and creditors so that only the corporation's assets are reachable by creditors. In order to make a corporation work, the incorporators must treat the corporation as a separate entity. It cannot simply act as the alter ego of the owner. All financial records must be maintained separate and apart from the owner's.

5. Eliminate Personal Guarantees.
Personal guarantees subject the assets of the guarantor to the creditor. Instead of providing a guarantee, ask the lender to accept a bond, insurance, or even the corporation's credit as security for the loan. Personal guarantees are very risky and should only be agreed to when there is no alternative.

> Personal guarantees are very risky...only agree to them when there is no other alternative.

6. Trusts.
There are a number of different kinds of irrevocable trusts which are used in income tax and estate planning. Certain trusts, known as "spendthrift" trusts, limit a beneficiary's right to transfer or pledge his or her interests. If a beneficiary cannot reach the assets of an irrevocable trust, then neither can his or her creditors.

7. Charitable Remainder Trusts.
In this type of trust the charities remainder interest (that which is left over) also is safe from the creditors of the person establishing the trust.

8. Offshore Trusts.
This is tricky. However, well-known places for establishing trusts where strong privacy and

debtor-protection laws exist include the Cook Islands and the Isle of Man. The key is what the foreign law says about where the property subject to the trust is located. Sometimes, the actual property can remain where it is (presumably in the United States) but often the property is required to be located in the jurisdiction where the trust is established. These instruments are very complex, very expensive and not much law interpreting the effect of the trust exists in the United States. Hire a competent tax lawyer. Do not rely on someone else's lawyer or the lawyer for your investment partners.

> Hire a competent tax lawyer if you're considering an offshore (foreign) trust.

9. Retirement Plans.

If you have an ERISA Qualified Retirement Plan or a KEOGH, these plans are unreachable by the employer's creditors or by the creditors of the individual participant in the plan. Remember that the retirement plan, in order to be protected, must be qualified and single-person pension plans usually held by professionals may be excluded.

10. IRAs

The law governing individual retirement accounts is your state's law. Some states offer complete protection against creditor claims; others exempt only those IRA funds which come from an ERISA Qualified Retirement Plan.

11. Insurance Funded Plans.

Funding a qualified retirement plan with insurance proceeds may also be of some value since some states' laws protect a life insurance and annuity contract from creditors. Also insurance funded non-qualified deferred compensation plans may also be protected under state insurance codes depending on the law in your state.

12. Welfare Benefit Trusts.
Welfare Benefit Trusts provide tax-favored severance, disability and death benefits. Protection is afforded to all trust assets under federal law against both participants, and employer's creditors.

13. Exemptions.
Every state has its own exemptions list that sets forth the property that creditors cannot take from debtors. For example, a "homestead" exemption for home equity exists in all states. Some states impose strict dollar limits on the amount of the exemption while other states do not.

> A "homestead" exemption for home equity exists in all states.

VI. Serious Financial Trouble and Credit Counseling

Unfortunately, some credit problems are not "temporary" or solvable by lifestyle and budget changes or asset protection. These financial problems are just too severe. You are probably experiencing serious financial difficulty if one or more of the following applies to you:

1. You cannot pay all of your monthly bills with all of the money you earn (your

take-home pay together with other income you receive after taxes, payroll deductions, and other expenses);

2. Your minimum credit card payments on all credit cards combined exceeds 25 percent of your net monthly earnings;

3. After all your monthly bills and expenses are paid, you do not have enough to put at least 5 percent into a savings account for future use;

You are probably experiencing serious financial difficulty if these situations apply to you.

4. You use credit to meet your monthly expenses;

5. You have depleted your savings and therefore must borrow to pay your income taxes, take a vacation or pay for other unforeseen expenses not covered in your monthly expense budget;

6. You are often late with payments to creditors, in arrears or you pay only the minimum required;

7. A legal judgment has been taken against you.

If you find yourself in one or more of these situations, consider using the services of a credit counselor. However, be careful! Credit counseling may be unregulated in your state. Some people claiming to be "credit counselors" are nothing more than salespeople for high interest credit cards or outright con artists. Deal only with reputable credit counselors. Check to see if you credit counselor has been **certified** by the National Certification Board of the National Foundation for Consumer Credit. This certification means that the counselor has demonstrated both a high level of competence and ethical fitness in the financial counseling field. One such consumer credit counseling service, which is nonprofit and sanctioned by the National Foundation for Consumer Credit, is Consumer Credit Counseling. They have offices in every state. I have worked with this group for years and highly recommend them. Their toll free number is 1-800-388-2227.

> If you hire a service, you will sign a legal document making the counseling service your trustee.

Most reputable and certified counseling agencies are funded by contributions from community businesses, including banks, hospitals, credit unions, individuals and various government grants. They are usually nonprofit services and charge only a nominal fee, say $15 to $25 per month, if you elect to use their services.

You will first meet with a counselor and discuss your personal finances. He or she will help you develop a monthly budget which will result in all of your creditors being paid over time. If you hire the service, you will sign a legal document making the counseling service your trustee. You will give the trustee your bills and he or she will pay them out of your monthly earnings, which you also will turn over to him for depositing into an account.

The counselor will work with you to establish an allowance to cover all of your personal expenses. He or she then will negotiate with your creditors for lower monthly payments, a waiver of interest and an agreement that the creditor will take no legal action or proceed with any further collection efforts, as long as you make your payments. The advantage to the creditor is that they get paid in full, eventually. The advantage to you is that you get control of your financial circumstances without resorting to bankruptcy.

VII. Bill Collectors and the Fair Debt Collection Practices Act

Do not consider filing for bankruptcy simply because you are being pestered by creditors. A federal law called the "Fair Debt Collection Practices Act" was passed in 1978 to prohibit certain methods of debt collection. The Fair Debt Collection Practices Act covers collection of any debt incurred for personal, family or household purposes. The Act applies to any person in the business of collecting debts owed to others (including lawyers who represent creditors) unless both are related by common ownership or control; any creditor who, collecting from his own debtors, uses a name other than his own; any one who regularly collects or attempts to collect debts for another (including attorneys).

> Do not consider filing for bankruptcy simply because you are being pestered by creditors.

Not all debt collectors are subject to the Act. It does not apply to banks, other lenders or businesses which collect their own accounts, using their own names, nor does it cover them when they collect an isolated debt for another.

A covered debt collector may contact a person other than the debtor only to discover or verify the debtor's location. In doing so, the collector must:

◊ identify himself, but he must identify his employer only if expressly requested to do so;

◊ not reveal the consumer's indebtedness to anyone other than the debtor;

◊ not use a post card or in way reveal debt collection activities;

◊ not communicate with that person more than once unless reasonably necessary.

Responsibility for enforcing the law is through the Federal Trade Commission and the courts through private lawsuits. If you wish to obtain forms for complaining about a particular debt collection practice, contact your local FTC office (address and phone numbers are at the end of this chapter) or an attorney.

Know your rights when dealing with debt collectors!

Debt collectors are forbidden by law from using harassing or abusive tactics such as:

◊ Threatening the use of force against you or threatening to damage your credit reputation;

◊ Using obscene or profane language;

◊ Telling you that they will make public your name as a "deadbeat" or someone who does not pay debts. (However, they have the right to report your delinquency or non-payment to a credit agency);

◊ Using the phone to intimidate or annoy;
◊ Using the phone without identifying themselves as debt collectors or as representatives of a creditor;
◊ Advertising your debt in a publication;
◊ Using false statements about who they are, for example, implying that they are attorneys or that they are law enforcement personnel and that you have committed a crime or that you will be arrested if you do not pay what is owed;
◊ Giving false credit information about you to anyone;
◊ Using a false or fictitious name in an effort to collect;
◊ Sending you documents that look like official court or government documents when they are not.

Under the law, a debt collector may contact you in person or by mail, telephone or telegram. But he or she may not contact you at inconvenient times or places. This means before 8 a.m. or after 9 p.m. A collector may not contact you at work if you tell him or her not to do so.

> A debt collector may not contact you at work if you tell him or her not to do so.

Within five days after contacting a debtor without paying a debt, the collector must send a written notice that includes the following information:

◊ the amount of the debt;
◊ the name of the creditor;
◊ that the debt will be assumed to be valid unless disputed within 30 days;

◊ that if disputed, the collector will verify it and send a copy of the verification or of a judgment against the consumer;

◊ that upon request the name and address of the original creditor (if changed) will be provided.

During the period when a debt is being verified, the collector may not attempt to obtain payment.

If you have a lawyer, the collector cannot contact you directly, but most go through your attorney. Generally, the collectors can contact others, but only to find out where you live or work. The debt collector is **prohibited** from telling anyone other than you or your lawyer that you are in debt, except in very limited special circumstances.

It is also illegal for a debt collector to collect more than you owe; or to deposit a post-dated check before the date on the check; or to send you postcards regarding your debt.

If the debt collector violates the Fair Debt Collection Practices Act, you may have the right to sue for damages in state or federal court if you bring your suit within **one year** from the date of the violation. The law allows you to recover your costs and reasonable attorney's fees in addition to any damages.

A debt collector who violates the Fair Debt Collection Practices Act is liable for statutory dam-

> If you have a lawyer, the collector cannot contact you directly, but must go through your attorney.

ages of up to $1,000, for each violation of the Act, rather than a total of $1,000 according to a ruling handed down by the Sixth Circuit in *Wright v. Finance Service of Norwalk* in 1993. In that case, the Plaintiff claimed that a debt collector committed thirty technical violations of the Act in the course of sending fourteen letters trying to collect a $112 medical bill. The court interpreted the law to say that the collector may be liable for up to $30,000 in statutory damages, plus actual damages, attorney's fees and costs.

> You should report problems with debt collectors to your state attorney general's office.

This decision will offer serious deterrent to some debt collectors who knowingly violate the Act as a business practice because they don't expect to incur significant liability. However, while statutory damages up to $1,000 for *each violation* are allowed, a court may, in its discretion, award less than the maximum. The Act sets forth a number of factors for a judge to consider in determining whether to impose the maximum allowed by the law, including the frequency and nature of the violation as well as the intent of the debt collector.

If others you know have been wronged by a single debt collector, then all of you may sue on a "class action" basis and recover damages of up to $500,000 or one percent of the collector's net worth, whichever is less.

You should also report problems with debt collectors to your state attorney general's office. Look in the telephone directory under state government for the attorney general's phone number. Most states have strong laws, in addition to the federal Fair Debt Collection Practices Act, which give you additional rights.

If you have a question about your rights under the Fair Debt Collection Practices Act, the Federal Trade Commission (FTC) may be able to help. The FTC cannot give you legal advice or act as your lawyer, but you may contact the FTC offices closest to you for more information.

FTC HEADQUARTERS

Federal Trade Commission
6th and Pennsylvania Avenue, N.W.
Washington, DC 20580
202-326-2222

FTC REGIONAL OFFICES

1718 Peachtree St., N.W.
Atlanta, GA 30367
404-347-4836

100 N. Central Expressway
Dallas, TX 75201
214-767-5503

10 Causeway St.
Boston, MA 02222-1073
617-565-7240

1405 Curtis St.
Denver, CO 80202-2393
303-844-2271

55 East Monroe Street
Chicago, IL 60603
312-353-4423

11000 Wilshire Blvd.
Los Angeles, CA 90024
213-575-7890

668 Euclid Avenue, Ste. 520A
Cleveland, OH 44114
216-522-4210

150 Williams St., 13th Fl.
New York, NY 10038
212-264-120

901 Market St.
San Francisco, CA 94103
415-995-5520

2806 Federal Bldg., 915 2nd Ave
Seattle, WA 98174
206-552-4656

VIII. How Credit Reporting Works

Remember, every time you buy something on credit a record is kept by the seller of how well you make your payments. The seller (your creditor) may report the history of your account to one or more of three national credit reporting agencies. They are: 1) Credit Data of America; 2) CBI/Equifax; and 3) TRW. Consult the Yellow Pages under "Credit Reporting Agencies" for the local address and phone number of each of these agencies.

> If you make a credit purchase, a record of your bill-paying habits is generated.

There are other local or regional agencies to which a creditor may report, but these three are the most common. Collectively they keep records on over 150 million American consumers.

The credit reporting agency does **not** rate you. It simply collects and holds information which it received from those who extend credit. The agencies hold three types of information: 1) personal history; 2) information contained in public records that relates to you; and 3) credit history. The credit reporting agency is **not authorized** to investigate you. The information they obtain regarding your personal life comes from what you have put on credit applications when you have attempted to obtain credit. This includes information concerning you, spouse, your pre-

41

sent and past employers, your social security number, date of birth, whether you own or rent, etc. The public record information comes from your county (or your parish if you live in Louisiana) records and usually consists of judgments which have been recorded against you, tax liens, mortgages, deeds of trust, security agreements and UCC filing statements. Records concerning any bankruptcy filings, even if you are not discharged, also may be kept by the credit reporting agency.

A consumer report may be issued only to properly identified persons for approved purposes.

The account information usually consists of the name of the creditor; the type and amount of credit extended; when the credit was extended; the payment history on the account, including any nonpayments or late payments. Most large creditors have a computer-originated reporting system, so this information is reported when the credit is initially extended and simply updated as payments are made or not made.

A consumer report about you may be issued only to properly identified persons for approved purposes. It may be furnished in response to a court order or in accordance with your own written request and it may be provided to someone who will use it in connection with the valuation of a credit transaction, employment, underwriting of insurance, determination of eligibility for a license or other benefit granted by a governmental agency, or other legitimate business need.

Obviously, your friends and neighbors who are curious about your affairs may not obtain information about you. To do so might subject the subscriber who obtained it for them to fine and/or imprisonment.

The Fair Credit Reporting Act gives every consumer the right to look at his or her file. If you are denied credit, you are entitled to a copy of your credit report from the agency that reported to the creditor who turned you down, for free, if you make the request within 30 days of the day you were turned down.

If you have not been turned down, but want to check the accuracy of the information the credit reporting agency has gathered about you, simply call or write the agency nearest you. There is a nominal fee for the report. Remember it is free **only** if you have been denied credit.

> If you are denied credit, you are entitled to a copy of your credit report...at no charge.

If you dispute the information, get a "dispute form" free of charge from the agency, fill it out, attach copies of any documents which you think prove or help prove that you made payments and send it back to the credit reporting agency, by U.S. Mail, return receipt requested. Also send a copy of this letter and the attachments to the creditor who reported the information you think is wrong, also by U.S. Mail, return receipt requested, asking that the creditor correct the record and report the correction to the credit reporting agency.

When you notify the credit bureau that you dispute the accuracy of information, it must reinvestigate and modify inaccurate data. Any pertinent data you have concerning an error should be given to the credit bureau immediately. If free investigation does not resolve the dispute to your satisfaction, you may enter a statement of 100 words or less in your file, explaining why you think the record is inaccurate.

The law, however, does not require that a credit bureau add to your credit file a statement of circumstances that explains a period of delinquency caused by some unexpected hardship, such as a serious illness, unemployment, or other problems. This type of information should be given by you directly to the credit grantor when applying for credit.

Be sure to keep copies of all letters that you send and receive from the agency.

The credit bureau must include your statement about disputed data, or some sort of coded version contained in their computer printout of it, with any reports it issues about you to the creditor seeking the information. At your request, the bureau must also send a correction to anyone who received a report in the preceding six months if it was for a credit check, or within a two-year period for employment purposes.

Do not try to correct errors in your credit record over the telephone. The credit reporting agency will not change records based on what you tell them over the phone. They must have written documentation. **Keep copies of your letters**.

Any consumer reporting agency or user of reported information who willfully or through negligence fails to comply with the Fair Credit Reporting Act provisions may be sued by the consumer. If the agency or the user is found responsible, the consumer may be awarded actual damages, court costs and attorney's fees, and, in the case of willful non-compliance, punitive damage is allowed by the court. The action must be brought within two years of the occurrence or within two years after discovery of material in willful misrepresentation of information. An unauthorized person who obtains a credit report under false pretenses may be fined up to $5,000, imprisoned for one year, or both. The same penalties apply to anyone who willfully provides information to someone not authorized to receive it.

> A person receiving a credit report under false pretenses may be fined, jailed or both.

Nine federal agencies share in the enforcement of the Fair Credit Reporting Act. If you wish to report a problem, you may contact the Banks Consumer Affairs Department for referral to the appropriate agency.

Two other consumer protection laws—the Fair Credit Billing Act and the Equal Credit Opportunity Act—also contain provisions relating to your credit history. The Federal Reserve Bank of Philadelphia provides two free pamphlets discussing these rights. You may write or call for them:

Federal Reserve Bank of Philadelphia
Department of Consumer Affairs—P.O. Box 66
Philadelphia, PA 19105-0066
215-574-6116

IX. Beware of "Credit Fixes!"

No one can clean up your credit record! There is no special ability credit services have to fix your credit. Credit services which claim they can do this for you by "erasing" or "repairing" your bad credit can do little more than what I have indicated above, and you can be sure that they will charge you dearly for their "service." While they may also offer you the opportunity to "establish" good credit with a MasterCard or other credit card without looking into your credit history, please note that this kind of credit card usually requires a pledge of some security on your part.

"Credit repair services" don't do much except charge a fat fee.

You can find out, on your own and without paying for the services of a credit "repair" agency, which banks will provide you with such credit cards (regardless of your credit background) without having to pay a fee to an agency. Write: Bankcard Holders of America, 560 Herndon Parkway, Ste. 120, Herndon, VA 22070, or call 703-481-1110. But be careful! Do you really need more credit? It is a serious mistake to get another credit card in order to use it to make debt payments or purchase more goods.

Please, beware of "debt consolidation" loans. Sometimes consolidation makes sense, but it is not a cure-all. Often the monthly payment on the consolidation loan, although lower than the collective total of your monthly payments on all of your credit obligations, involves a high interest rate which will stretch out your obligation years longer than you expect. You will be paying very little on the principal that you owe and a great deal of interest each month for a very long time. Interest, by the way, that is **no longer tax deductible**. Another problem with a debt consolidation loan is that it usually requires security. You may have to pledge the equity in your car or house to get the loan, since the pay-off will take longer. And, if you default, your consolidation loan creditor will have the right to take the security which you have pledged.

Lastly, a debt consolidation loan does not get you out of debt. It may result in a lower monthly payment overall, but **it puts you further into debt for a longer period of time**, while at the same time encumbering assets which you otherwise may have owned free and clear.

> It can be a serious mistake to get a credit card in order to make debt payments...
> ...think twice.

For more information about consolidation loans and second mortgage financing, write *"Facts for Consumers,"* Bureau of Consumer Protection, Federal Trade Commission, Washington, DC 20580. You may also wish to write for the FTC brochures on the Truth in Lending Act, The Equal Credit Opportunity Act, the Fair Credit Reporting Act and the Fair Debt Collection Practices Act.

X. What Is Bankruptcy and Why Are There Different Kinds?

The law calls the person trying to get help the "*debtor*" or "*petitioner*." Under the laws regulating what we commonly call "*bankruptcy*," the "*debtor*" or "*petitioner*" has certain rights which he may exercise that will result in the debtor not having to pay his or her debts. In going to court, the petitioner is asking for "*relief*" from these debts. The relief is called a "*discharge*." In other words, if all of the laws and procedures are followed, the debtor will receive a court order saying he or she never has to pay the debts he or she had when the petition was filed.

Filing for bankruptcy, or "petitioning the court in bankruptcy for relief from creditors," are two ways of saying the same thing. But since "filing for bankruptcy" is widely used in everyday language, I will use the same phrase in this book.

> In going to court, the petitioner is asking for "relief" from his debts.

The most common types of "voluntary" bankruptcy are: Chapter 7, Chapter 11, Chapter 12 and Chapter 13. **Voluntary bankruptcy** is where you, as opposed to your creditors, ask the court for relief. **Involuntary bankruptcy** is where the creditors force you into the bankruptcy court. Involuntary bankruptcy for individuals generally occurs when several creditors you have not paid think that they can force you to pay by bringing you to court and having a court-appointed trustee liquidate your assets and pay them.

Farmers and nonprofit corporations may not be forced into bankruptcy, although each may file **voluntary** bankruptcy. If you are served with a Petition for Involuntary Bankruptcy, call a lawyer immediately. If you do not, a default could be entered against you and drastic consequences could result.

The "chapters" in the names of the type of bankruptcy, such as "Chapter 7," refer to the chapters or sections of the United States Bankruptcy Code where the law about each kind of bankruptcy is found. Remember that bankruptcy law and the bankruptcy court procedures are governed by federal law. Certain matters in bankruptcy, like exemptions, may be determined by state laws, so that the rights of parties may vary from state to state.

Also, procedural rules may vary from state to state according to the local practices of the bankruptcy courts. This is another reason to get a lawyer if you are considering bankruptcy. There are many horror stories about people, just like you, who filled out the forms without a lawyer's help, only to lose their homes, their cars or other assets unnecessarily.

Certain matters in bankruptcy may be determined by state laws and thus vary from state to state.

XI. The Basic "Chapters" of Bankruptcy

Chapter 7—Chapter 7 is "straight liquidation." That is, your non-exempt assets are given to a court-appointed trustee who arranges to have them turned into cash and paid to your creditors. Sometimes there are no non-exempt assets, and no creditors are paid. Even if no creditors are paid, you are entitled to keep your exempt assets, and you should still be entitled to a discharge.

Chapter 11—Chapter 11 is a method of reorganization which usually does not involve liquidation or turning assets over to a trustee. A plan of reorganization must be approved by the court after it has been prepared by the debtor or a creditor. This type of bankruptcy usually is used by corporations, partnerships and, sometimes but less often, by individuals who are heavily in debt. These debtors need time to reorganize, but they eventually expect to be able to pay their creditors.

Chapter 12—Chapter 12 was created in 1986 specifically for family farmers who had too much debt to qualify for a Chapter 13-type filing. A farmer is likely to be eligible for relief if more than 50 percent of his or her income and 80 percent of his or her debts are from farming. The total debt must be under $1.5 million. The farmer must be able to show the court he or she has a stable enough income to make payments according to the court-approved plan.

Bankruptcy by any other name...

Chapter 13—Chapter 13 is known as the "poor man's Chapter 11." It is similar to Chapter 11 reorganization, except that it's designed for those who are "wage earners" or small business owners. If you have a regular income and certain specified debt limitations, Chapter 13 allows you to pay creditors on an installment basis according to a court-approved plan. You retain control of all of your assets, not just the "exempt" ones as in the case of a Chapter 7. Generally, your creditors are paid from money generated from your earnings, although the law allows payment from the sale of certain assets as well. ——

> The forms in the back of this book illustrate what information you're required to furnish when filing.

In Chapter 13, you may pay back some or all of your general creditors. Whether you are allowed to retain non-exempt assets depends on how much you pay back to creditors.

The wage earner recognition plan (Chapter 13) does not require creditors to vote on whether your plan is acceptable, as required in Chapter 11, but creditors can object to the plan. Creditors in Chapter 13 cases may be paid out of the debtor's future earnings **and** existing assets. If you choose this plan, you most likely will be using your future income to pay creditors, and you may be able to avoid liquidating all of your non-exempt assets.

I have included forms which are used for Chapter 7 filings in the back of the book, as an illustration of what kind of information you will be required to furnish if you file. This will give you an idea of the type of information your lawyer will need.

Since Chapter 7 and Chapter 13 are the most common types of bankruptcy for wage earners who are not farmers, each deserves a closer look.

XII. What Is Involved in a Chapter 7 and What Property Can I Keep If I File?

Chapter 7 requires liquidation of your non-exempt assets to pay creditors. Most of your debts will be discharged, but you do not get to decide which ones.

You must turn over all of your property to a trustee who is appointed by the court. You and your lawyer will prepare court papers claiming "exemptions." Certain property is considered "exempt" property. That is, if property is exempt, you may keep it even though you are also asking the court to relieve you from paying your debts. The idea behind exemptions is to let you keep what is necessary for a fresh start. This property is not taken by the trustee. He, who has no power to sell it and use the proceeds to pay creditors. One of the most important jobs your attorney has is helping you keep as much of your property exempt as the law allows. If it is exempt, then it is forever out of the control of the trustee and it is **not** part of your bankruptcy estate. Even though you keep it, you still are entitled to a discharge of your debts.

The idea behind "exemptions" is to let you keep what is necessary for a fresh start.

Federal bankruptcy law provides that each state may determine what property may be claimed as exempt in a bankruptcy case. A state **may** choose to allow its citizens to select the list of exempt property contained in the bankruptcy code, known as the "federal exemptions," or it may choose to "opt out" of the scheme of federal exemptions and have state laws dictate what property may be claimed as exempt. In the alternative, state law may direct that the debtor in bankruptcy can select either federal exemptions or the state created exemptions. **Accordingly, the property you may claim as exempt in a bankruptcy case will depend upon the law of the state in which you live, if you file in that state.**

> What is exempt is not the same everywhere. Contact a local licensed attorney to be sure!

The type of property that you may be able to claim as exempt is therefore not the same in every state. But, generally, the type of property considered exempt includes:

◊ Some equity in your home. (Ask your lawyer about "homesteading," which is a provision of **state** law providing protection of a homeowner's equity. By using the residence exemption from the bankruptcy law in connection with the state homestead provision, you may be able to keep your home);

◊ Some equity in your car;

◊ Some personal property such as furnishings, household goods, clothes, appliances, books, animals, crops and musical instruments used by you or your dependents;

◊ Tools, professional books used in trade/ business by you or your dependents;

◊ All unmatured life insurance contracts (no credit life);

◊ All professionally prescribed health aids for you or your dependents;

◊ Your right to receive Social Security benefits, unemployment compensation, veteran's benefits, disability/unemployment benefits, alimony and child support;

◊ You or your dependents' rights to receive payment under a state bonus, pension, profit sharing, annuity or similar compensation plan because of illness, disability, death, age or length of service (subject to technical exceptions);

◊ Your right to receive money from a victim crime law, if enacted in your state, wrongful death benefits and compensation for injuries.

Remember, the exemptions you are entitled to use may be different than these, depending upon your state's laws. Exemptions are constantly changing. You should contact a lawyer for the correct status on exemptions.

Know what your assets are...you may have more than you think!

All non-exempt assets must be made available to the trustee in a Chapter 7-type bankruptcy. The definition of "assets" is very broad. It includes anything of value that you have that is not designated by the law to be an exemption. As a practical matter, non-exempt property that has little value usually will not be sold by the trustee for the benefit of creditors. This type of property will, at some point, be **abandoned** from the estate by the trustee and, thereafter, remain your property, provided it is not the subject of a lien.

Obviously, your wages, personal property and cash in a bank are assets. But so is your right to sue someone for causing you bodily injury. The right to sell and distribute the proceeds from the sale of your assets always rests with the trustee.

If you keep exempt property that you still owe money on under some sort of installment plan, you will have to "reaffirm" the debt and bring the creditor current or lose the exemption and the asset. For example, if you owe $200 per month on your car loan, you may agree to **continue** making payments according to the terms of the original installment debt contract, and keep the car.

Pre-bankruptcy planning is allowed and is very important. But get a lawyer's help in this area.

In Chapter 7 cases, the law also allows you the option of "redeeming" tangible personal property intended primarily for personal, family or household use from a lien securing a dischargeable consumer debt by paying the lienholder the current fair market value of the item in one **lump sum**.

The law provides for exemptions, but the bankruptcy court makes the final decision on any question about what a debtor may claim as an exemption. If a creditor feels that an exemption you claim is not justified under the law, he or she has the right to file a document in court asking the judge to make a ruling on whether it is exempt or non-exempt.

Pre-bankruptcy planning is allowed by law. This means that you can convert non-exempt assets to exempt assets **before you file.** For example, if you have extra cash before filing, you may use that money to purchase an exempt asset. However, you must be careful! Pre-planning does not give you the right to avoid paying specific creditors. You need professional guidance in this area.

XIII. What Happens to My Non-Exempt Property in Chapter 7?

If there are any non-exempt assets left in your estate, the trustee sells them and uses the proceeds to pay the creditors. Who is paid, in what order, and how much depends on the law of priority established by federal statutes. The law provides six categories of unsecured claims which are to be paid. Secured creditors are usually "paid" by getting their security back. A creditor must go to court to get his security back; it cannot be done without your knowledge. You will have an opportunity to contest. As for non-secured creditors, the following claims are paid out of the proceeds of sale of your non-exempt assets in the following order:

> The law provides six categories of unsecured claims which are to be paid out of your assets.

◊ **Administrative Costs and Legal Fees.** The new changes to the bankruptcy law have liberalized this category to include attorney's fees. The court awards fees claimed by an attorney based upon the nature and extent of the value of the services rendered. In awarding fees, the court will focus on the difficulty of the case, the time your lawyer spent on your case, and the rates charged in your area by other lawyers for similar services. If your lawyer has employed a paralegal to help, the billings of the paralegal will be included as "professional fees."

The court will not give fees automatically. Your attorney must file a document in court stating the terms of payment with the client and any other modifications to the employment relationship concerning fees.

> These claims are paid out of the proceeds of the sale of your non-exempt assets in this exact order.

◊ **Unsecured Claims For Wages, Salary or Earnings.** This applies only to money earned within ninety days of the filing of the petition, up to a maximum of $2,000.

◊ **Unsecured Claims For Employee Benefits.** This refers to contributions your employer makes to any benefit plan (retirement, profit sharing, etc.) arising from your services performed for the employer within six months of your filing of your petition. This amount cannot exceed the total number of employees receiving contributions multiplied by $2,000, less any credit for wage claim.

◊ **Unsecured Claims of Farmers Against the Debtor.** This only applies if you own or operate a grain storage facility or a fish produce facility, and only up to $2,000.

◊ **Unused Claims of Deposit.** This applies to any deposit for purchase or lease of real property, or the purchase of services for private use that either did not close or were not received, up to a maximum of $900.

◊ **Unsecured Tax Claims.** There are seven types of claims which are paid last:

1. Income or gross receipt tax returns which are due within three years of the filing of the petition;
2. Real property taxes payable within one year before the filing of the petition;
3. Penalty taxes;
4. Exempt taxes due within three years before the filing of the petition;
5. Excise taxes;
6. Consumer debts on goods imported within one year before the filing of the petition;
7. Tax penalties.

XIV. What Is Involved in Chapter 13 and What Property Can I Keep If I File?

You may keep **all** of your property while the repayment plan is in effect. Sale of assets is usually not necessary. If you own a business, you may continue to operate the business.

As in the case of a Chapter 7 filing, the automatic stay is in effect so creditors cannot take **any** action to collect what you owe. During the proceedings, the court has the power to permit a reduction of payments required on secured debts. All payments in Chapter 13 are spread out according to a repayment plan.

> Relief from accelerated payments is available under Chapter 13.

Chapter 13 results in what some people call the "Super Discharge." This is because under Chapter 13, you may be discharged from debts which are **not** dischargeable under Chapter 7. For example, debts which resulted from fraud or intentional, malicious acts, and certain other debts may be discharged in a Chapter 13 proceeding. ___

Chapter 13 will not allow the discharge of long-term debts where the last payment is due after the end of the Chapter 13 plan of repayment. However, in the case of certain long-term debts like mortgages, where the lender has "accelerated" (that is, demanded that a greater portion or all of the remaining balance be paid sooner), Chapter 13 may allow you to stop the acceleration and reinstate the mortgage by bringing it current.

The Chapter 13 option requires repayment of your debts, usually over a period of **three years**. Under certain circumstances, this period may be lengthened to five years by order of the court. The court has the power to reduce the amount to be paid back and grant a discharge of the unpaid balance, except for secured debts and certain non-dischargeable debts like alimony, child support and certain taxes.

The plan is proposed by you and your lawyer and presented to the court. If approved by the court, unsecured creditors **must** accept it, provided that each creditor receives as much of the principal of the debt balance as he would if your property was liquidated (sold and the proceeds distributed to your creditors).

When the plan is approved by the court, you become obligated to make monthly payments according to the plan. If you cannot make these payments, the court may allow you to modify the plan. But in the event you are not permitted to modify, or if you are unable to make payments according to the plan approved by the court, you may still get a discharge by converting to a Chapter 7 liquidation.

XV. Which Is Best, Chapter 7 or 13?

If all else fails, you need to decide whether Chapter 7 or Chapter 13 bankruptcy is best for you. Chapter 7, or liquidation, discharges you from most of your debts, but you must relinquish any asset which is not exempt. In contrast, Chapter 13, or personal reorganization, involves a partial or complete payback of your debts to your creditors. So long as certain criteria are met, you are able to keep **all** of your property.

When to file Chapter 7.

Guidelines for When to File Chapter 7

◊ If six years have passed since your last Chapter 7 discharge, you are eligible to file;

◊ If you don't have any non-exempt property;

◊ If all of your unsecured debt is dischargeable (certain debts are not dischargeable, such as student loans or debts which were incurred as a result of fraud or malicious injury);

◊ If your income is insufficient to pay back any debts;

◊ If you are not anticipating incurring additional large debt in the near future;

◊ If you wish to surrender to the creditor any secured property on which you owe more than the value of the collateral.

Guidelines for When to File Chapter 13

◊ If you need relief from creditors, but are not eligible for Chapter 7. (You may file a Chapter 13, even if six years have not passed since you were discharged under Chapter 7);

◊ If you own non-exempt property. (You will need to pay back to unsecured creditors the value of the non-exempt property);

◊ If certain debts are non-dischargeable. (With the exception of certain taxes, alimony and child support, you can discharge debts that are non-dischargeable in Chapter 7, such as debts incurred by fraud, intentional or malicious acts);

Chapter 13 lets you keep your assets and pay your creditors over time.

◊ If you are in default on a secured loan and desire to keep the property. (You will be given a reasonable time to cure the default in Chapter 13);

◊ If you owe more than the value of secured property and desire to keep the secured property. (The fair market value of the secured property will determine the amount of the secured debt. The loan balance above and beyond the value of the property would simply be unsecured debt);

◊ If you own a business and wish to continue to operate the business;

◊ If you wish to modify the interest rate on certain high interest loans. (You can require that the secured creditor accept market value rate instead of the stated rate on the loan);

◊ If you owe non-dischargeable taxes. (Under Chapter 7, those taxes are not discharged, but in Chapter 13, you can pay them back over time and not have to pay accruing interest and penalties);

◊ If your income is far in excess of your normal monthly expenses. (If you have extra income, you have to file Chapter 13);

◊ If there is a possibility that you are going to incur additional unsecured debt in the near future. (You may be entitled to include that debt in your Chapter 13 even if it is incurred after the filing);

◊ If for personal or emotional reasons, you feel better at least trying to pay back creditors (it may be better for your credit also).

XVI. What Is Bankruptcy Court?

Each state has at least one "bankruptcy court" in each district of the United States. Bankruptcy courts are not part of the state court system. They are part of the United States District Court, but the bankruptcy judge, not a U.S. District Court judge (except in very limited matters involving personal injury and wrongful death suits) has the power to hear and decide bankruptcy matters. Look in the telephone directory under "Federal Government" or contact a licensed attorney. ___

Employees of the bankruptcy courts, including secretaries, clerks, etc., cannot give you legal advice.

Please note that the employees of the bankruptcy courts, including secretaries, clerks, etc., are **not** lawyers. They may be able to answer your questions concerning where to file, how the filing fee is to be paid, but they will not give you legal advice or help you fill our your petition or schedules. Do not waste your time trying to get a bankruptcy court clerk or secretary to tell you what to do. Severe penalties, including loss of job, may result if any employee attempts to give legal advice to someone filing for bankruptcy. Besides, since they are not lawyers, it is not wise for you to accept their advice.

XVII. Who May File Bankruptcy?

Individuals, partnerships and corporations may petition the bankruptcy court for relief. In the case of individuals who are married, it is permissible for only one spouse to file. In a state which has "community property" law, if only one spouse files and receives a discharge, the individual debts of the filing spouse are discharged as to that spouse's share of community debts. Both husband and wife may file together in a joint petition which requires the payment of only one filing fee.

XVIII. What Are the Steps in Going to Bankruptcy Court?

Petition and Fees. The process begins with the filing of a "Petition for Relief" with the clerk of the bankruptcy court in the jurisdiction where you have lived or worked during the six months before the filing. You also must pay a filing fee when you file, which is $120 for Chapters 7 and 13; $500 for Chapter 11. Chapter 12 requires a $200 fee. If you cannot afford to pay the fee, you must ask the court, in a signed, written application filed with your petition, for permission to pay the fee in installments. You must state the reason and avow to the court that you have not paid your attorney yet. The filing fee **must** be paid in full within four months, or, in unusual circumstances, six months.

A section in the back of this publication contains forms used in bankruptcy court. These forms are for Chapter 7, or straight liquidation. Although these forms are official, they are **not** the correct size and **cannot be used** for the actual filing in bankruptcy court. However, by familiarizing yourself with them, you will know what information and documents you need in order to prepare your petition.

> The forms in the back of this book are official, but are not the correct size. Don't attempt to file them.

There is no law which requires that a person have a lawyer in order to file a petition or appear in court. Most states, however, require corporations and partnerships to be represented by lawyers. This is true even in the case of a corporation where all of the shares of the corporation are owned by only one or two people.

Even though you are not required to have a lawyer in order to file a petition, **it is strongly recommended.** Remember, court procedures must be **followed exactly**. If you act as your own attorney, you will be held to the same professional standards as a practicing lawyer. The court will not give you "a break" because you did not have a lawyer or because you were acting as your own lawyer. The rule is that you are **presumed** by the judge to know as much about the law as a lawyer, and you will be treated that way in court if you handle your own case.

> Court procedures must be followed exactly!

If you do something wrong in court, even unintentionally, or if you forgot about or did not know about a certain rule, the court could, depending on what it is that you did, throw out your case. Do you really want to be your own lawyer?

Automatic Stay. At the time you file your petition, your creditors are prevented, by law, from trying to collect their debts. This is the result of what is called an "Automatic Section 362 Stay." "Stay" is a legal term meaning that **all** attempts by a creditor to collect from you must stop the moment the petition is filed or severe penalties may be levied by the court against the creditor. While no sheriff or other person goes to each of your creditors to tell them that a stay is in effect, the law provides that the mere act of your filing forces creditors to stop collection efforts.

Since the stay is **automatic** with the filing of the petition, you and your lawyer need not take any further action for it to take effect. The court will send notice of your filing to all of your creditors so that they are aware that you are in bankruptcy. You have to notify only those creditors who are likely to take action to seize your property before you file.

If a creditor takes some action against you, like garnishment, attachment or execution after the petition has been filed, that action is voidable, that is, it may (and usually will) be declared to have **no legal effect.** If it can be shown that the creditor knew you had filed your petition but disregarded the stay and did something to try to collect the debt, the court will probably void whatever action the creditor has taken and may hold the creditor in contempt. The court also has the power to award attorney's fees and your out-of-pocket expenses attributable to the creditor's violation of the stay.

"Stay" is a legal term meaning that all attempts by a creditor to collect from you must stop.

Creditors' Statements and Schedules. The clerk of the bankruptcy court will not accept your petition if you do not have a complete list of all of your creditors and their correct addresses. Within 15 days of the filing of your petition, you must file a schedule and a statement of affairs. These documents form the basis of the court's understanding of your assets, debts and exemptions.

It is of the utmost importance that you list **all** of your creditors, their correct addresses, and **all** of your debts in your petition! If you do not, you risk losing a discharge of that debt. Only debts contained on the schedules may be discharged unless it can be shown the creditor had actual knowledge of the pending bankruptcy.

List all of your assets even if you think your creditor is not interested in pursuing the debt or even if you **dispute** the debt. Old debts, partially paid debts, or debts which are only contingent, that is, they depend on something occurring which has not yet occurred at the time of the filing, must be listed. The simple rule of thumb is, when in doubt, list the creditor and the debt.

> It's important that you list all of your creditors, their addresses, and all of your debts in your petition.

If you remember a creditor or debt that you had forgotten to include on your petition when filed, the law allows you to "amend" or add the debt and the name and address of the creditor to the schedule. The definition of "debt" is very broad. It includes **anyone** to whom you owe money. Do not forget to list things that you may not think are debts, such as child support or spousal maintenance payments. Other financial obligations, such as past-due taxes and debts secured by collateral which already have been repossessed also must be included.

In Chapter 7 cases, you also will need to sign a "Statement of Intention." This relates mainly to credit card or other consumer debt. In this document you must tell your consumer goods creditors whether you want to keep the property for which you are still paying. You have a choice. You can **surrender the property**, that is, give it back; or you can keep it. If you keep it, you must **reaffirm** the debt. That is, you must say in writing that you will continue to make payments, since this debt will not be discharged. Similarly, in Chapter 7 cases, you may **redeem** personal property used primarily for personal, family or household purposes, if you pay its fair market value in a lump sum.

When to File. Please note that the timing of the filing of the petition is very important, For example, your right to a tax refund which accrues before you file will become property of your bankruptcy estate. In Chapter 7, the income you earn or other assets you receive before filing all goes to the trustee. The income you receive after the filing is yours, if it is for services performed by you after the filing, except for any inheritance you actually received within 180 days of your filing.

The timing of the filing of the petition is very important.

If you receive payment after filing a Chapter 7 petition for services performed prior to the filing, the income received belongs to the bankruptcy estate (except to the extent that it is exempt). If you are paid for work performed both before and after the filing of the petition, there may have to be an apportionment between you and the estate.

Matrix. The master mailing list which consists of all of your creditors by name and address is put on a grid so that mailing labels can be made by the court staff. The court uses this "matrix" to send notice to all of your creditors about hearings and other actions which occur during your case. Copies of all of the court's rulings in your case will be sent to all those who are on the matrix. The creditors can contest your discharge and take other action permitted by law. When a creditor takes such action, he or she is required to give you, the trustee and the court, as well as all of the other creditors, notice.

First Meeting of Creditors. Shortly after you file for bankruptcy, the court sends notice to all the creditors you have included in your petition and tells them that a stay is in effect. The court also gives them notice of a first meeting of creditors and a deadline for them to file their claim. The first meeting of creditors is usually held about 30 days from filing of the petition. **You will have to go to court**, take the witness stand and swear, under oath, that the petition and schedules are correct. You also will state under oath that you have not filed for bankruptcy relief in any court during the last six years.

> The first meeting of creditors is usually held within 30 days of the filing of the petition.

The questions are asked of you by your lawyer or the trustee's representative. Then, your creditors have a chance to ask you questions. Often creditors do not come to this meeting. There is no requirement that they be there, and in cases where there are no assets, it is highly unlikely that a creditor will appear. The proceedings are held on the record and are recorded. Generally, the proceeding lasts five to ten minutes, but depending on the court in your jurisdiction, there may be a number of creditors' meetings scheduled for the same time or within minutes of each other. Waiting to be called could take up to half a day or more.

If a creditor does come to ask questions, it is likely that he or she will ask questions concerning the location of various assets or other matters which are contained in the papers you have filed.

If you fail to get a discharge, you will be required to continue to pay.

The trustee or lawyers for the creditors also may take your deposition. That is, they may ask you to come to their offices to answer questions **under oath** before a court reporter. This is an unusual proceeding in cases of straight liquidation (Chapter 7) or in cases where there are no non-exempt assets. When a creditor requests a deposition, he probably is looking for or exploring the basis of any objection he may have to your discharge. Remember, the creditors want to be paid. If it appears to the creditor, from something that he has learned or something you have stated in your petition, that there are grounds to oppose your discharge, then he may do so. If you fail to get a discharge, **you will be required to continue to pay** or he can get a judgment against you, which can then be used to seize your assets. For example, a creditor may learn that you have lied about your income or debts on a MasterCard application. This misrepresentation or fraud could be grounds for non-discharge of that MasterCard debt. In order to get the judge to rule that the debt is not to be discharged (and that you still must pay the creditor) the creditor can take your deposition about these facts. The creditor would then have a record he could use as a basis for asking the judge to declare the debt nondischargeable.

A trustee is usually an experienced professional, but does not have to be a lawyer.

Appointment of a Trustee. In Chapter 7 cases, an "interim" or temporary trustee is appointed soon after you file your petition and pay your fees. In Chapter 11, there is no trustee appointed automatically, but creditors may ask to have one appointed. In such cases, you are considered the trustee and "debtor in possession." In Chapter 11 and Chapter 13 cases, you retain control of all of your assets. However, in a Chapter 7 proceeding, the trustee will collect your non-exempt assets and determine how to pay your creditors according to law. Although the trustee is empowered to collect non-exempt assets, she may not always do so. **The trustee may choose to abandon such assets from the estate.** Sometimes there are no non-exempt assets and creditors receive nothing.

A trustee is usually an experienced professional but does not have to be a lawyer. A trustee's main job is to reduce the non-exempt assets to cash in order to pay creditors. A trustee also considers creditors' claims. In the case of any objection or dispute between the creditor and the debtor, the bankruptcy court judge, not the trustee, hears both sides and makes a decision. The trustee may make choices and recommendations affecting claims, but the bankruptcy court judge makes the final decision if there is a dispute.

Proof of Claim. A "proof of claim" is a written document filed by a creditor with the court describing the creditor's claim. Creditors do not have to file proofs of claim in Chapter 11 reorganization bankruptcies because the debtor's schedules, which have been filed with the court by the debtor (you) are presumed to be correct. However, creditors in Chapter 11 cases must file proof(s) of claim if the debts listed are disputed, contingent, or unliquidated. In Chapter 7 or Chapter 13, creditors must file proofs of claim, or they may lose their right to make any claim later. If a creditor files a proof of claim, it is considered valid unless you object by filing a written objection with notice to all parties.

Certain creditors may not contest any of the proceedings, even with grounds to do so.

Creditors' Rights. During the course of the proceedings, your creditors have opportunities to assert claims against you. They may try to use the law to get paid in full. Certain creditors may not contest any of the proceedings, even if they have good grounds to contest your discharge. This depends upon the policy of the creditor and the amount of the debt. For example, where the debt is small, say under $1,000 or where there are no assets, creditors will probably not bother to contest your discharge, even if you misrepresented your income (which could be grounds for nondischarge of that debt) because the cost of hiring an attorney, preparing the appropriate court documents and arguing the matter in court is likely to cost them much more than what they could recover if they are successful. In such situations, creditors usually have a policy about whether they will pursue the matter. However, **they have a right to pursue it** and you cannot be sure that they will not.

Avoiding Transfers. If you transfer assets to others to avoid having to turn them over to the trustee, you run the risk of not receiving a discharge. Giving your assets to someone else without getting reasonable value back or in order to hinder, delay or prevent a creditor from obtaining a valid debt is likely to be considered a **fraudulent conveyance**. The court has the power to recover such transfers, even if you made them up to within one year before you file your petition. That property is then liquidated and given to your creditors.

> Be careful about giving away your assets before you file!

Similarly, if you pay a greater amount on some debts before filing, the court may recover what you paid. This is called a "preference." It is a payment made to benefit certain creditors at the expense of others, and gives that creditor more money than he would receive from his fair and proportionate share from your liquidated assets. Paying bills in the normal course of business is not grounds for recovering the payment.

Stay Lift Motions. Because an automatic stay is in effect the moment you file your petition, a creditor cannot take **any action whatsoever** trying to collect his debt from you. This means he cannot sue you, write letters to you, or contact you to get you to pay. But, the creditor can file a paper in court asking the judge to "lift the stay." By filing this paper, the creditor is trying to get the judge to rule or allow the creditor to continue efforts to collect the debt. If a creditor does file such a motion, he must notify you, and you will have to respond in writing. A hearing also is set, if it is requested, at which time you and the creditor may present any testimony or offer any exhibits which help the judge make his decision to lift the stay or leave it in effect.

> A creditor cannot sue you, write letters to you, or contact you to get you to pay.

In most cases, the stay is not lifted unless the creditor can show that the debtor has no equity in the property and that the property is not important to the bankruptcy estate. For example, if you own a lot which is encumbered by a mortgage or deed of trust and the amount you owe on the loan you took out to buy the property is equal to or greater than the fair market value of the lot, you have no equity in the property and the court might lift the stay. The idea is that if there is no equity, there is no asset value in the property for your estate; so the bankruptcy court should not protect it. When the stay is lifted, the creditor is allowed to exercise what rights he may have under state law.

So, if the creditor is entitled to repossess the property, he may now do so. Or, if he is entitled to foreclose a lien on the property, such as conducting a trustee's sale, he may proceed with the sale. If the stay is lifted, it affects only that particular creditor and that particular property.

To avoid the possibility of a lift stay, you can give your creditors additional protection by: 1) agreeing to pay cash amounts to your trustee to satisfy the obligation; 2) giving the creditor a lien; or 3) negotiating an agreement with the creditor so that he gets the equivalent of his interest in the property.

If a motion to lift the stay is filed, the court must make its decision within thirty days or the stay is considered to be lifted regarding the property which is the subject of the motion to lift stay.

XIX. What Is a "Discharge" and When Is One Granted?

The most important result of choosing the bankruptcy option, drastic as it may be, is that it will result in a "discharge" or a court order excusing you from paying the debts you had at the time you filed your petition. The bankruptcy discharge eliminates personal liability on pre-petition debts, but it does not eliminate liens on property unless they are specifically avoided in the bankruptcy case. If a timely complaint objecting to the entry of the discharge has been filed, the court will not enter a discharge order until after the proceeding is resolved.

A "discharge" is a court order excusing you from the debts you had at the time you filed your petition.

If you have complied with all of the requirements of the law, then the law provides that you are entitled to a discharge as a matter of right. If you have filed a Chapter 7 case, you will be given a discharge usually within three to five months after your filing. But it could take longer depending upon such things as the docket backup of the court or how complete your schedules have been prepared.

If you have elected to proceed in Chapter 12 or Chapter 13, which outlines a method of flexible repayment of some debt instead of liquidation of all of your assets, you also will receive discharge from your debts, except for consumer debt you incurred after the filing of the petition, spousal maintenance and child support. Chapter 11 discharge is not broader than the discharge in Chapter 7. **Chapter 13 discharge offers an expanded discharge and permits discharge of many debts, excluding certain types of alimony and child support, that are not dischargeable in Chapter 7 or 11.**

XX. Types of Debt You'll Still Have to Pay Even If You Get a Chapter 7 or Chapter 11 Discharge

The bankruptcy law provides that you will remain liable for certain debts even if you have received a discharge. **You will still be liable for the following debts even if you get a discharge under Chapter 7 or Chapter 11.**

1. Taxes owing within three years before you filed your petition.

2. Credit you obtained by filling out a false credit application. "Luxury" credit card or consumer debt incurred within 40 days before you filed which totals, from all sources, more than $500 or cash advances totalling, from all sources, more than $1,000 incurred within 20 days before you filed.

3. Willful or intentional damages you caused someone else. For example, if someone is suing you because you beat him up and put him in the hospital, this obligation would not be discharged or wiped out because beating up somebody is an "intentional act." The bankruptcy law also says that if you are being sued because you were involved in an automobile accident in which you were driving while intoxicated, there can be no discharge of the damages you caused the other party while you were driving drunk. However, in a situation where you are simply "negligent," the discharge will wipe out any judgment which is taken against you; you will not have to pay for the other person's damages even where it is your fault. The law requires a creditor to file a complaint about this within sixty days from the first meeting of creditors. If he or she does not, this debt also will be discharged.

4. Spousal maintenance (alimony) and child support payments.

5. Debts which you did not disclose in the papers you filed with the court, even if you just forgot and did not intend to leave the creditor out. But, the creditor must file a timely complaint or these will be discharged.

6. Fines or penalties you owe to any governmental agency (for example, an IRS late-filing penalty).

7. Any financial obligations that are your responsibility because of fraud. Whenever a creditor wants to prevent you from being discharged because he claims you made false statements to him getting credit, or he claims that you outright defrauded him, the creditor must file a written statement to that effect and send a copy to you within ninety days of the first meeting of creditors. If he does not, he loses his right to object to your discharge. It is the bankruptcy judge, and not the trustee, who decides whether there was fraud or falsity in connection with the debt and also decides whether a discharge is appropriate.

It is important to note that if a creditor claims you defrauded him and misrepresented facts and he is wrong, and the court also finds that the legal position which he has taken is not substantially justified, you may be **entitled to recover** your costs and attorney's fees involved in proving the creditor wrong. The court also has the power to order the creditor to pay any out-of-pocket losses you have incurred in proving the creditor wrong, such as lost wages for having to take off work to come to court to testify. Please keep in mind that under the most recent changes in the bankruptcy law, if you give a false statement to a creditor, only the debt which came from the statement will be non-dischargeable. Under the old law, any false financial statement was grounds to prevent a discharge as to all debts.

8. Educational loans taken out within five years of filing. There is a hardship exception, however.

9. Claims from an earlier bankruptcy. Once you have been discharged, you may not petition the court for bankruptcy again until six years have passed. If six years pass and you file again, the debts you were supposed to pay in the first bankruptcy will not be discharged. In other words, the second bankruptcy does not erase the obligations that were left over from the first bankruptcy.

XXI. Reasons Why the Court Will Not Give You a Discharge

There are some cases in which the law will **not** permit a debtor to be discharged at all. There are ten circumstances which will prevent you from being discharged.

1. The debtor is not an individual. In other words, generally a corporation is not permitted to receive a discharge in Chapter 7. Corporations or partnerships are not permitted to have "fresh starts." A corporation or partnership may be reorganized or it may be liquidated, but it usually does not receive a discharge from the bankruptcy court.

2. The debtor has purposely destroyed property to mislead creditors. If you have, within one year before or after the filing of the bankruptcy petition, destroyed, concealed or transferred any property with the intent of hindering, delaying or defeating your creditors and/or the bankruptcy court, there will be no discharge.

3. The debtor has failed to keep adequate records. All of the books and financial records concerning your financial condition must be kept up to date and accurate. If the court or the trustee cannot figure out your finances, or where there is so much uncertainty as to what your true financial condition is and you have been given an opportunity to produce the records which would clarify it and have not, you will not be discharged.

4. The debtor has lied under oath or has attempted a bribe. Suffice it to say that bribes are a crime and, in connection with bankruptcy, they will prevent your discharge. Similarly, if the debtor has lied under oath there will be no discharge. Lying under oath includes lying in court (on the witness stand) and lying in the petition. Don't say or write anything that is not the complete truth.

5. The debtor has failed to explain the loss of assets. The trustee will want to know, and is entitled to know, why you may have lost certain assets. You can expect that a thorough explanation will be required.

Please keep in mind that I am not talking about having to explain why you are in bankruptcy court in the first place. You will not be refused a discharge simply because you made stupid mistakes, made poor investments or were careless with credit. But you **will** be denied a discharge if you fail to explain where an asset is after having been ordered and given the opportunity to do so. You will be subject to civil penalties, as well as criminal penalties for perjury if you lie.

If your losses are related to criminal acts for which you could be prosecuted, you have a right to remain silent. This right against self incrimination is given to all citizens through the Fifth Amendment of the U.S. Constitution and can be exercised at any time. You **must get an attorney** for advice on what to do in such circumstances. It may be possible, for example, for an attorney to obtain "immunity" from prosecution for you so that you can freely answer questions without fear of criminal punishment. However, this is complicated and involves serious legal consequences for you. If you are involved in criminal activity, get a lawyer now.

6. The debtor has disregarded a lawful Court Order. From time to time the court may order you to do certain things, such as produce certain records or answer certain questions. A refusal to obey any lawful order of a bankruptcy judge or to answer any reasonable question which relates to your financial condition will prevent discharge. The only exception is where your answers to the questions would tend to incriminate you, or where the judge's order was wrong.

7. The debtor has filed for bankruptcy before. A debtor may not file for bankruptcy within six years of the earlier petition. If he has, there will be no discharge. This applies only to obtaining a Chapter 7 discharge, after a discharge has been granted under Chapter 11, 12, or 13. This limitation does not necessarily apply to consecutive Chapter 11 or consecutive Chapter 13 cases.

8. The debtor has filed for bankruptcy before, but has not received a discharge and has done an act described in Sections 2 through 6 above. Some people have filed bankruptcy before but have not received a discharge; either the petition has been dismissed or thrown out. If a person has done so or can be shown to have committed any of the acts in Sections 2 through 6 above, discharge will not be granted.

9. The debtor has been discharged in a Chapter 13 proceeding within the previous six years and less than 70 percent of the total was paid to his creditors. Remember, Chapter 13 is "reorganization" rather than "liquidation," which is Chapter 7.

10. The debtor has submitted a written Waiver of Discharge and obtained court approval. This is where the debtor agrees to give up, or waive his right to a discharge, and the court has signed an order permitting waiver after Chapter 7 has been filed.

XXII. How Do I Know If I Should Petition for Protection of the Bankruptcy Court?

Sometimes you will not be able to negotiate with your creditors. Sometimes credit counselors cannot help you either. Since success in negotiating depends upon the willingness of the creditor to voluntarily negotiate a longer period of repayment, a creditor does not have to agree to accept less than what is owed, and may wish to exercise her right to collect all to which she is entitled. Whether she also is entitled to compound interest, court costs, and attorney's fees depends upon the written terms of the loan agreement you signed when you applied for your credit card or loan. If the creditor wants all that the law allows, she probably will get it, depending upon how determined she is. She could get a legal judgment against you, garnish your wages or lien your house.

You should not file a bankruptcy petition until you have discussed your situation with a qualified attorney.

If you have been sued and a sizeable judgment has been taken against you, it is extremely unlikely that a judgment creditor (the person with the court judgment which allows him to claim a right to get money from you) will agree to take small monthly payments. However, you should not file a bankruptcy petition until you have discussed your situation with a qualified and licensed attorney. In certain severe cases, bankruptcy is the only way to stop a creditor from taking your property and getting control of your finances. But it should be only a last resort.

XXIII. What Are the Drawbacks to Bankruptcy?

Bankruptcy is like strong medicine—it can help make you well, but there are powerful side effects. Bankruptcy is the single most devastating thing you can do to your credit reputation. Too often, what is thought of as an easy way out becomes a financial nightmare that devastates your credit reputation. Since bankruptcy is a matter of public record, you and your family must be prepared to live with the discomfort which comes from others knowing that you have filed for bankruptcy. You also must be prepared to face your creditors and others in court and tell them that you are unable to handle your own finances, or reveal an illness or layoff which has proven insurmountable.

> Bankruptcy can and probably will remain on your credit record for up to ten years.

Bankruptcy can, and probably will, remain on your credit record for up to **ten years**. Credit reporting agencies typically keep bankruptcy records for that long. However, even after ten years, when the bankruptcy is erased from your credit report, most credit applications ask, "Have you ever taken bankruptcy?" You may then be asked to disclose all of the circumstances surrounding your earlier filing. This could result in credit denial.

While there is no rule of law preventing some creditor from making a loan to you or extending credit to you after you have been involved in a bankruptcy, creditors may believe that you are too big a risk and not extend credit. Those people who file bankruptcy are likely to feel its effects for their entire lives.

Keep in mind that once you file bankruptcy, you face the very real possibility of having to live without credit. In this day and age we take credit for granted. Without credit, you may be forced to pay cash for **all** of your purchases. This may not appear to be a problem to you because you may be thinking that if you don't have to pay your present debts, paying cash will not be difficult. But what happens if you are forced to relocate to another part of the country? Can you afford to pay cash for the move? Can you afford to pay cash for a new home? Can you afford to pay cash for a new car or unexpected major repairs?

> Once you file for bankruptcy, you may have to live without credit.

After being involved in a bankruptcy, credit may be offered to you. However, it is usually offered at above-market rates, meaning that you will be required to pay much more interest. A creditor also may want security in other property that you own. If you accept, you can be sure that a creditor will keep a close watch on your account and take advantage of all of the power the law gives him to take away the security you have provided him in the event you are late with payments or fail to make payments when due.

This raises another problem. How can you create or build your new asset base after it has been liquidated in bankruptcy? If you have filed a Chapter 7 bankruptcy and some of your assets are sold for the benefit of creditors, it may be very difficult to accumulate what you had without using credit.

Don't forget to consider the costs involved in filing!

Finally, the costs and fees of filing for bankruptcy relief must be considered. Attorneys charge according to the complexity of the case. Fees are different in different parts of the country. Generally, attorney fees range from $300 to $1,200 for Chapter 7 personal bankruptcy cases. Higher fees are charged for more complex cases which involve more work. Lawyer fees also vary from place to place, as do the fees charged by the court appointed trustee who will administer your assets while you are in Chapter 7. Trustee fees may add several hundred dollars more to the cost of the bankruptcy. Attorney fees for Chapter 11 and Chapter 13 cases are much higher.

XXIV. What Do I Gain By Filing Bankruptcy?

The most important benefit of bankruptcy is that it gives you a "fresh start." It also prevents creditors from taking any action against you while the case is in court. If you are granted a discharge, creditors are prevented from taking action against you after the case ends. You also may get to keep some, if not most, of your assets, **if** they are exempt when you file a Chapter 7 liquidation case. If all the rules are followed, the court will order that you are legally free from paying the debts you had when you filed your petition. Depending on the circumstances, you may not have to give up your house, your car, your tools, etc. Depending upon the law, you may be discharged from paying your debts and still keep some or all of your important assets.

> The most important benefit of bankruptcy is that it gives you a "fresh start."

Most people try their best to pay their bills and usually succeed. But, unexpected expenses such as an uninsured illness, death, divorce or disability can create financial havoc in one's personal finances.

Remember, always try to avoid bankruptcy first by informing your creditors of the reasons you cannot pay, and then by negotiating with them for lower payments spread over time without interest. Be sure to use the Fair Debt Collection Practices Act to stop any harassment. Get the help of a licensed credit counselor before you consider bankruptcy. If your financial crisis is temporary, or if your credit is good, bankruptcy should be avoided if at all possible.

If you still cannot resolve your financial crisis using these techniques, explain your situation to a licensed and experienced bankruptcy attorney. Carefully review with him your finances and ask his advice on whether bankruptcy is **necessary** to resolve your problem. Only after you have thoroughly explored all your options should you file your petition.

Once you hire an attorney, **do not** hold anything back! Remember, she is there to help you and anything you tell her is "privileged." That communication **cannot** be divulged to anyone, even in court to a judge, without your consent, unless your conversation with the lawyer included **anticipated** illegal acts on your part. So, if you already have committed fraud or hidden your assets, tell the lawyer so she can begin to help you deal with it. There are some limitations to this attorney-client privilege, so be sure your lawyer knows that you want all necessary steps taken to preserve the confidentiality of what you tell her during your conference. Besides, lawyers have "heard everything." The lawyer won't think you are a fool or a terrible person for being in a tough spot. However, what you don't tell her can and will hurt your case, eventually. You can never tell your lawyer too much about your case.

> Tell your lawyer everything—she's "heard everything" already!

Use this book in preparing for your meeting with a credit counselor or lawyer. Be prepared by gathering the documents and information asked for in the petition and schedules found at the back of this book.

Since this book cannot possibly answer all of the questions you may have about your rights, organize your questions after you have carefully read and considered the materials contained throughout it. That way you can better use the professional's training and "get more for your money."

Some lawyers do not charge for an initial consultation, but many charge their customary rates, $80 to $250 per hour. Make sure you know what you will be charged **before** your first meeting. If you do not know a lawyer, contact your local, county or state bar association. Most have a "lawyer's referral" number which you can call to find a lawyer nearest to you who is experienced in bankruptcy matters.

> Lawyers are most effective when they are given enough time to "treat the disease."

Finally, lawyers, like doctors, are most effective when they have time to "treat the disease." The quicker you contact a licensed attorney, the sooner he can help. Waiting too long may decrease the willingness of creditors to work with you. Waiting too long also could prevent you from exercising some of the rights available to you under the law. Waiting also could cause you to lose valuable pre-bankruptcy planning opportunities. This is one case in which an ounce of prevention is worth a pound of cure.

XXV. If You Decide to File Chapter 7

On the following pages you will find the forms which you will be required to fill out if you file a Chapter 7 petition. I have included them because these forms show you the kind of information necessary to prepare court papers.

If you have made the decision to file, look over these forms carefully and gather the information requested **before** you see your lawyer.

Being fully prepared in advance of your meeting with your lawyer will help him tremendously in his effort to help you.

These forms are **examples** of the actual forms used in bankruptcy court, exact copies of what is used in court. However, they are not the right size, and in their present state cannot be accepted for use in any bankruptcy court for filing purposes. **Do not attempt to use them in court.**

> Remember that the forms in this book are just examples ...do not attempt to use them in court.

These forms are the current bankruptcy forms revised and approved by bankruptcy courts effective August 1, 1991. As this book goes to press, a dramatic overhaul of the bankruptcy code is being considered by Congress and stands an excellent chance of being enacted. New changes in the bankruptcy laws would:

◊ allow many additional individuals and sole proprietorships to file under Chapter 13;
◊ expand the ability of bankrupt homeowners to keep their homes;
◊ require bankrupt companies to fund their pension obligations before paying off other creditors;
◊ add protection to alimony and support debts;
◊ create a new, special procedure for small business bankruptcies which would be tried out in eight districts; and
◊ make a number of other changes.

It is interesting that these changes were contained in a similar bill which almost became law in 1992. That bill passed both the Senate and the House, but the conference version was killed in the last moments of the session when a filibuster on an unrelated measure kept it from coming to the Senate floor.

The new bill now stands a much better chance of being enacted. The House is taking up the proposal four months earlier than it had taken up the last bill, which should give Congress time to enact it during the 1994 session.

If the bill is passed, some of the forms which you are about to review will probably be changed and the law affecting bankruptcy will be substantially changed. **It is therefore of the utmost importance that you contact a bankruptcy lawyer before making any decisions which affect your legal position in order to determine what the bankruptcy code changes, if any, are.**

> If you cannot afford an attorney, see if one will represent you on a "pro bono" basis.

In the event that you are unable to afford an attorney and you are unable to qualify for legal aid (a free lawyer to help you file your bankruptcy petition), try contacting lawyers who practice in the bankruptcy courts to see if they will represent you on a **"pro bono"** basis. This means you are asking a lawyer to take your case for free. Some lawyers will do this simply because they believe that it is their obligation to help as many citizens as possible, regardless of their ability to pay.

However, if you have exhausted all of these attempts to get legal help, you have an absolute right to represent yourself in bankruptcy court. You cannot "represent" a corporation, even if you are its only shareholder. But, you are permitted by law to file your own bankruptcy petition, and represent yourself in all of the bankruptcy court proceedings.

If you decide to file without a lawyer, you can use these forms to help prepare your petition. In order to get the actual forms that can be used in court, you can purchase a "kit" which contains detailed instructions on how to fill out the forms; it is available at many bookstores and stationery stores. You also may obtain the forms directly from the bankruptcy court or a document preparation service.

> The law permits you to file your own petition, but you cannot file for anyone else or your company.

If you choose to represent yourself, you will have to draft your own petition. I recommend that you hire a document preparation service to help with the typing. Document preparation services are new and fulfill a limited but very important service—they will take the information you have prepared in longhand on sample forms and transfer it to official court documents. In other words, they save you the steps of having to obtain the forms and type them. A document preparation service has the forms necessary for filing in your jurisdiction. Simply tell them what should be contained in each section of the petition, or give them your notes, and they will type it up in the proper form and give it back to you to take to the bankruptcy court clerk's office for filing.

Take the typed originals which you have signed, along with five copies (the document preparation service also can make copies for you) and the filing fee in the form of a cashier's check in the amount of $120 to the clerk of the bankruptcy court. The person at the clerk's desk will stamp the date and the time on the papers, take your check and "log in" your petition on the docket with its docket number. **Be sure to keep a copy** of everything that you file along with documents from the court or anything else relevant to your case while your petition is being processed.

If you have documents prepared by a service, ask them about their "re-draft" policy.

When you have your documents prepared by a document preparation service, be sure to ask about their policy concerning "redrafts." In the event that you have improperly filled out the form, the court or the trustee may request that you do it over. Most reputable document preparation services will not charge you a fee for this redraft. Simply make the changes, have it redrafted by the service, and refile. You do not pay any additional filing fees to the court, unless the court has dismissed your petition, and you should not have to pay any more to the document preparation service.

Please remember that document preparation services, while very valuable, **cannot provide legal advice**. They cannot tell you to put in certain information nor can they explain to you the purpose of the information or how the court will view it. Remember, once you make the decision to represent yourself, you are truly on your own and cannot rely on bankruptcy court personnel, document preparation services or your friends for legal advice. Of course, you are always free to hire an attorney at any time, even after a petition is filed. Sometimes lawyers will agree to simply review your documents or help you over a hurdle that crops up, probably on an hourly basis. But this is not the rule, since most lawyers like to handle the case from start to finish.

> You may hire an attorney at any time, but most lawyers like to handle a case from start to finish.

A document preparation service should be able to give you directions to the bankruptcy clerk's office when you're ready to file the petition. The service also should be able to tell you about any additional forms that are used in your particular jurisdiction. Although the bankruptcy courts all follow the same general procedures, they are free to make "local rules" that do not conflict with the general law of bankruptcy court procedures. Be sure to ask for **all** the forms which are necessary to file the petition, including forms necessary to comply with local rules. No "local" forms are included in the section which follows.

XXVI. Chapter 7 Sample Forms

Review the sample forms carefully in order to learn what information to gather. If you are representing yourself, you can find the law pertaining to bankruptcy in the United State Code, Title 11. Ask your local librarian to help you find 11 U.S.C. §§ 101-1330. The law is indexed and the chapter heading should direct you to the aspect of the bankruptcy law with which you are interested. The forms are self explanatory. Remember that the bankruptcy law will probably change in the summer of 1994!

If you wish to proceed on your own, you might consider purchasing a kit, complete with detailed instructions. One such kit publisher is Alpha Publications of America, Inc. You can obtain their kit by writing to P.O. Box 13881, Tucson, Arizona 85732-3881. For further information, you may call them at 1-800-528-3494. Be sure to order the kit with the new changes from Sen. Howell Heflin's bill, S. 540.

You also may use a document preparation service to help prepare your forms for filing. You may obtain forms directly from their office. But get the new forms!

Please remember that the forms that follow are reduced copies of the actual forms. Although the forms found in this book are accurate in every respect, and the most recent forms used in bankruptcy court (approved August 1, 1991), they will not be accepted by any bankruptcy court for filing purposes because of their size.

BANKRUPTCY PETITION COVER SHEET

CASE NUMBER (Court Use Only)

INSTRUCTIONS: This form must be completed by the debtor or the debtor's attorney and submitted to the clerk of court upon the filing of the petition.

NAME OF DEBTOR (Last, First, Middle)	NAME OF JOINT DEBTOR (Spouse) (Last, First, Middle)
ALL OTHER NAMES, INCLUDING TRADE NAMES, USED BY THE DEBTOR IN THE LAST 6 YEARS	ALL OTHER NAMES, INCLUDING TRADE NAMES, USED BY THE JOINT DEBTOR IN THE LAST 6 YEARS
SOCIAL SECURITY NO. AND OR EMPLOYER'S TAX ID NO	SOCIAL SECURITY NO. AND OR EMPLOYER'S TAX ID NO
ADDRESS OF DEBTOR (Street, City, State, and Zip Code)	ADDRESS OF JOINT DEBTOR (Street, City, State, and Zip Code)
NAME OF COUNTY	NAME OF COUNTY

CHECK PROPER BOXES

TYPE OF PETITION

☐ Voluntary Petition   ☐ Involuntary Petition

CHAPTER OF THE BANKRUPTCY CODE UNDER WHICH THE PETITION IS FILED (Check One Box)

☐ Chapter 7   ☐ Chapter 11 Railroad
☐ Ch. 7 Broker   ☐ Chapter 12
☐ Ch. 9   ☐ Chapter 13
☐ Chapter 11   ☐ Sec. 304

CHECK DOCUMENTS FILED WITH PETITION:

☐ Statement of Affairs   ☐ Notice To Individual Debtors
☐ Summary of Schedules   ☐ Attorney's Disclosure of Comp
☐ Schedules A through J   ☐ List of 20 Largest Unsecured Crdtrs
☐ Statement of Intention   ☐ Chapter 13 Plan Analysis
☐ Corporate Resolution   ☐ Summary Of Chapter 13 Plan
☐ Exhibit A   ☐ Chapter 13 Plan
☐ Exhibit B   ☐ Master Mailing List

☐ ALL DOCUMENTS FILED

NATURE OF DEBT

☐ Business – Complete A, B, C below   ☐ Non-business Consumer

A. FORM OF ORGANIZATION (Check One Box)

☐ Individual   ☐ Partnership
☐ Corporation Publicly Held   ☐ Corporation Closely Held

B. TYPE OF BUSINESS (Check One Box)

☐ Farmer   ☐ Transportation   ☐ Construction
☐ Professional   ☐ Manufacture Mining   ☐ Real Estate
☐ Retail Wholesale   ☐ Other Business

C. BRIEFLY DESCRIBE NATURE OF BUSINESS

FILING FEE (Check One Box)

☐ Filing Fee Attached   Filing fee to be paid in installments by individuals only. Must attach signed application for the court's consideration indicating that the debtor is unable to pay fee except in installments. Rule 1006(b)

FOR ESTIMATES

ESTIMATED NUMBER OF CREDITORS					
1-15	16-49	50-99	100-999	1000-over	
☐	☐	☐	☐	☐	

☐ No assets will be available for distribution to creditors

☐ Assets will be available for distribution to creditors

ESTIMATED ASSETS (IN THOUSANDS OF DOLLARS)				
Under 50	50-99	100-499	500-999	1000-over
☐	☐	☐	☐	☐

ESTIMATED NUMBER OF EMPLOYEES- CHAPTER 11 AND 12 ONLY				
0	1-19	20-99	100-999	1000-over
☐	☐	☐	☐	☐

ESTIMATED LIABILITIES (IN THOUSANDS OF DOLLARS)				
Under 50	50-99	100-499	500-999	1000-over
☐	☐	☐	☐	☐

ESTIMATED NO. OF EQUITY SECURITY HOLDERS–CH. 11 & 12 ONLY				
0	1-19	20-99	100-999	1000-over
☐	☐	☐	☐	☐

ATTORNEY FOR THE DEBTOR (Firm Name, Address, Tel. No.) OR THE PETITIONER (IF INVOLUNTARY PETITION)

☐ No Attorney

NOTE: THIS PETITION WILL BE DISMISSED IF YOU FAIL TO FILE REQUIRED DOCUMENTS BY FIRST MEETING DATE OR IF YOU FAIL TO APPEAR AT THE FIRST MEETING

SIGNATURE OF ATTORNEY	DATE

FOR COURT USE ONLY

TRUSTEE: _____   341 HEARING   LOC _____   D&R HEARING   LOC _____
I J C P   BUS   CRED _____   DATE/TIME _____ _____   DATE/TIME _____ _____
COUNTY CODE   (CONF HEARING IF CHP 13)

UNITED STATES BANKRUPTCY COURT

_____ DISTRICT OF _____

In re

)

Debtor(s).

)

CASE NO. _____

CHAPTER _____

NOTICE TO INDIVIDUAL CONSUMER DEBTORS

The purpose of this notice is to acquaint you with the Four Chapters of the Federal Bankruptcy Code under which you may file a Bankruptcy Petition. The Bankruptcy Law is complicated and not easily described. Therefore, you should seek the advice of an attorney to learn of your rights and responsibilities under the law should you decide to file a petition with the Court. Neither the Judge nor the Court's employees may provide you with legal advice.

Chapter 7: Liquidation ($120 Filing Fee)

1. Chapter 7 is designed for debtors in financial difficulty who do not have the ability to pay their existing debts.

2. Under Chapter 7 a Trustee takes possession of your property. You may claim certain of your property as exempt under governing law. The Trustee then liquidates the property and uses the proceeds to pay your creditors according to priorities of the Bankruptcy Code.

3. The purpose of filing a Chapter 7 case is to obtain a discharge of your existing debts. If, however, you are found to have committed certain kinds of improper conduct described in the Bankruptcy Code, your discharge may be denied by the Court, and the purpose for which you filed the Bankruptcy Petition will be defeated.

4. Even if you receive a discharge, there are some debts that are not discharged under the law. Therefore, you may still be responsible for such debts as certain taxes and student loans, alimony and support payments, debts fraudulently incurred, debts for willful and malicious injury to a person or property, and debts arising from a drunk driving judgment.

5. Under certain circumstances you may keep property that you have purchased subject to a valid security interest. Your attorney can explain the options that are available to you.

Chapter 13: Repayment Of All Or Part Of the Debts Of an Individual With Regular Income ($120 Filing Fee)

1. Chapter 13 is designed for individuals with regular income who are temporarily unable to pay their debts but would like to pay them in installments over a period of time. You are only eligible for Chapter 13 if your debts do not exceed certain dollar amounts set forth in the Bankruptcy Code.

2. Under Chapter 13 you must file a plan with the Court to repay your creditors all or part of the money that you owe them, using your future earnings. Usually the period allowed by the Court to repay your debt is three years, but not more than five years. Your plan must be approved by the Court before it can take effect.

3. Under Chapter 13, unlike Chapter 7, you may keep all your property, both exempt and non-exempt, as long as you continue to make payments under the plan.

4. After completion of payments under your plan, your debts are discharged except alimony and support payments, certain kinds of taxes owed for less than three years, and long term secured obligations.

Chapter 11: Reorganization ($500 Filing Fee)

Chapter 11 is designed primarily for the reorganization of a business but is also available to consumer debtors. Its provisions are quite complicated, and any decision for an individual to file a Chapter 11 Petition should be reviewed with an attorney.

Chapter 12: Family Farmer ($200 Filing Fee)

Chapter 12 is designed to permit Family Farmers to repay their debts over a period of time from future earnings and is in many ways similar to a Chapter 13. The eligibility requirements are restrictive, limiting its use to those whose income arises primarily from a family owned farm.

CLERK OF THE BANKRUPTCY COURT

By _____

ACKNOWLEDGMENT

I(We), the undersigned debtor(s) hereby declare that I(we) have read this Notice To Individual Consumer Debtor(s) and understand the availability of relief under each of the four (4) Chapters of the Bankruptcy Code, as described above.

Dated: _____

_____
Debtor

_____
Joint Debtor

UNITED STATES BANKRUPTCY COURT

_____ DISTRICT OF _____

In re

)
)   CASE NO _____
)
)   CHAPTER _____
                          Debtor(s).   )   **APPLICATION TO PAY FILING FEES**
)   **IN INSTALLMENTS**
_____

In accordance with Federal Rules of Bankruptcy Procedures, Rule 1006, application is made for permission to pay the filing fee on the following terms:

$ _____ with the filing of the petition, and the balance of

$ _____ in _____ installments, as follows:

$ _____ on or before _____

$ _____ on or before _____

$ _____ on or before _____

$ _____ on or before _____

I certify that I am unable to pay the filing fee except in installments. I further certify that I have not paid any money or transferred any property to an attorney or any other person for services in connection with this case or with any other pending bankruptcy case and that I will not make any payment or transfer any property for services in connection with the case until the filing fee is paid in full.

Date: _____

                                              _____
                                              Applicant

                                              _____
                                              Co-Applicant

                                              _____
                                              Address

                                              _____
                                              City/State/Zip Code

ORDER

IT IS ORDERED that the debtor pay the filing fee in installments on the terms set forth in the foregoing application.

IT IS FURTHER ORDERED that until the filing fee is paid in full the debtor shall not pay, and no person shall accept, any money for services in connection with this case, and the debtor shall not relinquish, and no person shall accept, any property as payment for services in connection with this case.

BY THE COURT

Date: _____   _____

© 1991. ALPHA PUBLICATIONS OF AMERICA. INC — P.O. BOX 13881 — TUCSON. ARIZONA 85732-3881   FORM ABK-4001

UNITED STATES BANKRUPTCY COURT

_____ DISTRICT OF _____

In re

CASE NO. _____

Debtor(s)

**CHAPTER 7 INDIVIDUAL DEBTOR'S(S')
STATEMENT OF INTENTION**

1. I(We), the debtor(s), have filed a schedule of assets and liabilities which includes consumer debts secured by property of the estate.

2. My(Our) intention with respect to the property of the estate which secures those consumer debts is as follows:

    a. _Property to Be Surrendered._

Description of Property	Creditor's Name
1.	
2.	
3.	

    b. _Property to Be Retained. (Check applicable statement of debtor's(s') intention concerning reaffirmation, redemption, or lien avoidance.)_

Description of property	Creditor's name	Debt will be reaffirmed pursuant to § 524(c)	Property is claimed as exempt and will be redeemed pursuant to § 722	Lien will be avoided pursuant to § 522(f) and property will be claimed as exempt
1.				
2.				
3.				
4.				
5.				

3. I(We) understand that § 521(2)(B) of the Bankruptcy Code requires that I(we) perform the above stated intention _within 45 days_ of the filing of this statement with the court, or within such additional time as the court, for cause, within such 45-day period fixes.

Date: _____

_____
Signature of Debtor

_____
Signature of Co-Debtor

© 1991, ALPHA PUBLICATIONS OF AMERICA, INC.—P.O. BOX 13881—TUCSON, ARIZONA 85732-3881   FORM ABK-5001

Name of Debtor _____

Case No. _____

FILING OF PLAN

For Chapter 9, 11, 12 and 13 cases only. Check appropriate box

☐ A copy of debtor's proposed plan dated _____ is attached

☐ Debtor intends to file a plan within the time allowed by statute, rule or order of the court

PRIOR BANKRUPTCY CASE FILED WITHIN LAST 6 YEARS (If more than one, attach additional sheet)		
Location Where Filed	Case Number	Date Filed

PENDING BANKRUPTCY CASE FILED BY ANY SPOUSE PARTNER, OR AFFILIATE OF THE DEBTOR (If more than one, attach additional sheet)		
Name of Debtor	Case Number	Date
Relationship	District	Judge

REQUEST FOR RELIEF

Debtor requests relief in accordance with the chapter of title 11, United States Code specified in this petition

SIGNATURES

ATTORNEY

X _____

Signature   Date

INDIVIDUAL JOINT DEBTOR(S)	CORPORATE OR PARTNERSHIP DEBTOR
I declare under penalty of perjury that the information provided in this petition is true and correct	I declare under penalty of perjury that the information provided in this petition is true and correct and that the filing of this petition on behalf of the debtor has been authorized
X _____ Signature of Debtor	X _____ Signature of Authorized Individual
Date	Print or Type Name of Authorized Individual
X _____ Signature of Joint Debtor	Title of Individual Authorized by Debtor to File this Petition
Date	Date

EXHIBIT "A" (To be completed if debtor is a corporation, requesting relief under chapter 11)

☐ Exhibit "A" is attached and made a part of this petition

TO BE COMPLETED BY INDIVIDUAL CHAPTER 7 DEBTOR WITH PRIMARILY CONSUMER DEBTS (See P.L. 98-353 § 322)

I am aware that I may proceed under chapter 7, 11, 12, or 13 of title 11, United States Code, understand the relief available under such chapters, and choose to proceed under chapter 7 of such title

If I am represented by an attorney, Exhibit "B" has been completed

X _____

Signature of Debtor   Date

X _____

Signature of Joint Debtor   Date

EXHIBIT "B" (To be completed by attorney for individual chapter 7 debtor(s) with primarily consumer debts)

I, the attorney for the debtor(s) named in the foregoing petition, declare that I have informed the debtor(s) that (he, she, or they) may proceed under chapter 7, 11, 12, or 13 of title 11, United States Code, and have explained the relief available under such chapters

X _____

Signature of Attorney   Date

UNITED STATES BANKRUPTCY COURT

_____ DISTRICT OF _____

In re

CASE NO. _____

CHAPTER _____

STATEMENT OF FINANCIAL AFFAIRS

_____
Debtor(s).

Set forth all names including married, maiden and trade names used by debtor(s) within last 6 years. Also, Social Security Number(s) and all Employer's Tax Identification Numbers.

This statement is to be completed by every debtor. Spouses filing a joint petition may file a single statement on which the information for both spouses is combined. If the case is filed under chapter 12 or chapter 13, a married debtor must furnish information for both spouses whether or not a joint petition is filed, unless the spouses are separated and a joint petition is not filed. An individual debtor engaged in business as a sole proprietor, partner, family farmer, or self-employed professional, should provide the information requested on this statement concerning all such activities as well as the individual's personal affairs.

Questions 1 - 15 are to be completed by all debtors. Debtors that are or have been in business, as defined below, also must complete Questions 16 - 21. Each question must be answered. If the answer to any question is "None," or the question is not applicable, mark the box labeled "None." If additional space is needed for the answer to any question, use and attach a separate sheet properly indentified with the case name, case number (if known), and the number of the question.

DEFINITIONS

"_In business._" A debtor is "in business" for the purpose of this form if the debtor is a corporation or partnership. An individual debtor is "in business" for the purpose of this form if the debtor is or has been, within the two years immediately preceding the filing of this bankruptcy case, any of the following: an officer, director, managing executive, or person in control of a corporation; a partner, other than a limited partner, of a partnership; a sole proprietor or self-employed.

"_Insider._" The term "insider" includes but is not limited to: relatives of the debtor; general partners of the debtor and their relatives; corporations of which the debtor is an officer, director, or person in control; officers, directors, and any person in control of a corporate debtor and their relatives; affiliates of the debtor and insiders of such affiliates; any managing agent of the debtor. 11 U.S.C. § 101(30).

---

1. Income from employment or operation of business

None
☐

State the gross amount of income the debtor has received from employment, trade, or profession, or from operation of the debtor's business from the beginning of this calendar year to the date this case was commenced. State also the gross amounts received during the two years immediately preceding this calendar year. (A debtor that maintains, or has maintained, financial records on the basis of a fiscal rather than a calendar year may report fiscal year income. Identify the beginning and ending dates of the debtor's fiscal year.) If a joint petition is filed, state income for each spouse separately. (Married debtors filing under chapter 12 or chapter 13 must state income of both spouses whether or not a joint petition is filed, unless the spouses are separated and a joint petition is not filed.)

AMOUNT   SOURCE

2. Income other than from employment or operation of business

None State the amount of income received by the debtor other than from employment, trade, profession, or operation of the
☐ debtor's business during the two years immediately preceding the commencement of this case. Give particulars. If a joint
petition is filed, state income for each spouse separately. (Married debtors filing under chapter 12 or chapter 13 must state
income for each spouse whether or not a joint petition is filed, unless the spouses are separated and a joint petition is not
filed.)

AMOUNT   SOURCE

---

3. Payments to creditors

None a. List all payments on loans, installment purchases of goods or services, and other debts, aggregating more than $600 to
☐ any creditor, made within 90 days immediately preceding the commencement of this case. (Married debtors filing under
chapter 12 or chapter 13 must include payments by either or both spouses whether or not a joint petition is filed, unless the
spouses are separated and a joint petition is not filed.)

NAME AND ADDRESS OF CREDITOR	DATES OF PAYMENTS	AMOUNT PAID	AMOUNT STILL OWING

None b. List all payments made within one year immediately preceding the commencement of this case to or for the benefit of
☐ creditors who are or were insiders. (Married debtors filing under chapter 12 or chapter 13 must include payments by either
or both spouses whether or not a joint petition is filed, unless the spouses are separated and a joint petition is not filed.)

NAME AND ADDRESS OF CREDITOR AND RELATIONSHIP TO DEBTOR	DATE OF PAYMENTS	AMOUNT PAID	AMOUNT STILL OWING

---

4. Suits, executions, garnishments and attachments

None a. List all suits to which the debtor is or was a party within one year immediately preceding the filing of this bankruptcy
☐ case. (Married debtors filing under chapter 12 or chapter 13 must include information concerning either or both spouses
whether or not a joint petition is filed, unless the spouses are separated and a joint petition is not filed.)

CAPTION OF SUIT AND CASE NUMBER	NATURE OF PROCEEDING	COURT AND LOCATION	STATUS OR DISPOSITION

None b. Describe all property that has been attached, garnished or seized under any legal or equitable process within one year
☐ immediately preceding the commencement of this case. (Married debtors filing under chapter 12 or chapter 13 must include information concerning property of either or both spouses whether or not a joint petition is filed, unless the spouses are separated and a joint petition is not filed.)

NAME AND ADDRESS OF PERSON FOR WHOSE BENEFIT PROPERTY WAS SIEZED	DATE OF SEIZURE	DESCRIPTION AND VALUE OF PROPERTY

---

5. Repossessions, foreclosures and returns

None   List all property that has been repossessed by a creditor, sold at a foreclosure sale, transferred through a deed in lieu
☐ of foreclosure or returned to the seller, within one year immediately preceding the commencement of this case. (Married debtors filing under chapter 12 or chapter 13 must include information concerning property of either or both spouses whether or not a joint petition is filed, unless the spouses are separated and a joint petition is not filed.)

NAME AND ADDRESS OF CREDITOR OR SELLER	DATE OF REPOSSESSION, FORECLOSURE SALE, TRANSFER OR RETURN	DESCRIPTION AND VALUE OF PROPERTY

---

6. Assignments and receiverships

None a. Describe any assignment of property for the benefit of creditors made within 120 days immediately preceding the
☐ commencement of this case. (Married debtors filing under chapter 12 or chapter 13 must include any assignment by either or both spouses whether or not a joint petition is filed, unless the spouses are separated and a joint petition is not filed.)

NAME AND ADDRESS OF ASSIGNEE	DATE OF ASSIGNMENT	TERMS OF ASSIGNMENT OR SETTLEMENT

None b. List all property which has been in the hands of a custodian, receiver, or court-appointed official within one year
☐ immediately preceding the commencement of this case. (Married debtors filing under chapter 12 or chapter 13 must include information concerning property of either or both spouses whether or not a joint petition is filed, unless the spouses are separated and a joint petition is not filed.)

NAME AND ADDRESS OF CUSTODIAN	NAME AND LOCATION OF COURT CASE TITLE & NUMBER	DATE OF ORDER	DESCRIPTION AND VALUE OF PROPERTY

7. Gifts

List all gifts or charitable contributions made within one year immediately preceding the commencement of this case, except ordinary and usual gifts to family members aggregating less than $200 in value per individual family member and charitable contributions aggregating less than $100 per recipient. (Married debtors filing under chapter 12 or chapter 13 must include gifts or contributions by either or both spouses whether or not a joint petition is filed, unless the spouses are separated and a joint petition is not filed.)

NAME AND ADDRESS OF PERSON OR ORGANIZATION	RELATIONSHIP TO DEBTOR IF ANY	DATE OF GIFT	DESCRIPTION AND VALUE OF GIFT

8. Losses

List all losses from fire, theft, other casualty or gambling within one year immediately preceding the commencement of this case or since the commencement of this case. (Married debtors filing under chapter 12 or chapter 13 must include losses by either or both spouses whether or not a joint petition is filed, unless the spouses are separated and a joint petition is not filed.)

DESCRIPTION AND VALUE OF PROPERTY	DESCRIPTION OF CIRCUMSTANCES AND, IF LOSS WAS COVERED IN WHOLE OR IN PART BY INSURANCE, GIVE PARTICULARS	DATE OF LOSS

9. Payments related to debt counseling or bankruptcy

List all payments made or property transferred by or on behalf of the debtor to any persons, including attorneys, for consultation concerning debt consolidation, relief under the bankruptcy law or preparation of a petition in bankruptcy within one year immediately preceding the commencement of this case.

NAME AND ADDRESS OF PAYEE	DATE OF PAYMENT, NAME OF PAYOR IF OTHER THAN DEBTOR	AMOUNT OF MONEY OR DESCRIPTION AND VALUE OF PROPERTY

© 1991, ALPHA PUBLICATIONS OF AMERICA, INC. — P O BOX 13881 — TUCSON, ARIZONA 85732-3881   FORM ABK-6004

10. Other transfers

None ☐ a. List all other property, other than property transferred in the ordinary course of the business or financial affairs of the debtor, transferred either absolutely or as security within one year immediately preceding the commencement of this case. (Married debtors filing under chapter 12 or chapter 13 must include transfers by either or both spouses whether or not a joint petition is filed, unless the spouses are separated and a joint petition is not filed.)

NAME AND ADDRESS OF TRANSFEREE, RELATIONSHIP TO DEBTOR	PAYMENTS DATE	DESCRIBE PROPERTY TRANSFERRED AND VALUE RECEIVED

11. Closed financial accounts

None ☐ List all financial accounts and instruments held in the name of the debtor or for the benefit of the debtor which were closed, sold, or otherwise transferred within one year immediately preceding the commencement of this case. Include checking, savings, or other financial accounts, certificates of deposit, or other instruments; shares and share accounts held in banks, credit unions, pension funds, cooperative, associations, brokerage houses and other financial institutions. (Married debtors filing under chapter 12 or chapter 13 must include information concerning accounts or instruments held by or for either or both spouses whether or not a joint petition is filed, unless the spouses are separated and a joint petition is not filed.)

NAME AND ADDRESS OF INSTITUTION	TYPE AND NUMBER OF ACCOUNT AND AMOUNT OF FINAL BALANCE	AMOUNT AND DATE OF SALE OR CLOSING

12. Safe deposit boxes

None ☐ List each safe deposit or other box or depository in which the debtor has or had securities, cash, or other valuables within one year immediately preceding the commencement of this case. (Married debtors filing under chapter 12 or chapter 13 must include boxes or depositories of either or both spouses whether or not a joint petition is filed, unless the spouses are separated and a joint petition is not filed.)

NAME AND ADDRESS OF BANK OR OTHER DEPOSITORY	NAMES AND ADDRESSES OF THOSE WITH ACCESS TO BOX OR DEPOSITORY	DESCRIPTION OF CONTENTS	DATE OF TRANSFER OR SURRENDER, IF ANY

13. Setoffs

List all setoffs made by any creditor, including a bank, against a debt or deposit of the debtor within 90 days preceding the commencement of this case. (Married debtors filing under chapter 12 or chapter 13 must include information concerning either or both spouses whether or not a joint petition is filed, unless the spouses are separated and a joint petition is not filed.)

NAME AND ADDRESS OF CREDITOR	DATE OF SETOFF	AMOUNT OF SETOFF

14. Property held for another person

List all property owned by another person that the debtor holds or controls.

NAME AND ADDRESS OF OWNER	DESCRIPTION AND VALUE OF PROPERTY	LOCATION PROPERTY

15. Prior address of debtor

If the debtor has moved within the two years immediately preceding the commencement of this case, list all premises which the debtor occupied during that period and vacated prior to the commencement of this case. If a joint petition is filed, report also any separate address of either spouse.

ADDRESS	NAME USED	DATES OF OCCUPANCY

The following questions are to be completed by every debtor that is a corporation or partnership and by any individual debtor who is or has been, within the two years immediately preceding the commencement of the case, any of the following: an officer, director, managing executive, or owner of more than 5 percent of the voting securities of a corporation; a partner, other than a limited partner, of a partnership; a sole proprietor or otherwise self-employed.

*(An individual or joint debtor should complete this portion of the statement **only** if the debtor is or has been in business, as defined above, within the two years immediately preceding the commencement of this case.)*

16. Nature, location and name of business

None   a. If the debtor is an individual, list the names and addresses of all businesses in which the debtor was an officer, director,
☐   partner, or managing executive of a corporation, partnership, sole proprietorship, or was a self-employed professional within the two years immediately preceding the commencement of this case, or in which the debtor owned 5 percent or more of the voting or equity securities within the two years immediately preceding the commencement of this case.

b. If the debtor is a partnership, list the names and addresses of all businesses in which the debtor was a partner or owned 5 percent or more of the voting securities, within the two years immediately preceding the commencement of this case.

c. If the debtor is a corporation, list the names and addresses of all businesses in which the debtor was a partner or owned 5 percent or more of the voting securities within the two years immediately preceding the commencement of this case.

NAME	ADDRESS	NATURE OF BUSINESS	BEGINNING AND ENDING DATES OF OPERATION

17. Books, records and financial statements

None   a. List all bookkeepers and accountants who within the six years immediately preceding the filing of this bankruptcy case
☐   kept or supervised the keeping of books of account and records of the debtor.

NAME AND ADDRESS	DATES SERVICES RENDERED

None   b. List all firms or individuals who within the two years immediately preceding the filing of this bankruptcy case have
☐   audited the books of account and records, or prepared a financial statement of the debtor.

NAME	ADDRESS	DATES SERVICES RENDERED

None   c. List all firms or individuals who at the time of the commencement of this case were in possession of the books of
☐   account and records of the debtor. If any of the books of account and records are not available, explain.

NAME   ADDRESS

None   d. List all financial institutions, creditors and other parties, including mercantile and trade agencies, to whom a financial
☐   statement was issued within the two years immediately preceding the commencement of this case by the debtor.

NAME AND ADDRESS   DATE ISSUED

18. Inventories

None   a. List the dates of the last two inventories taken of your property, the name of the person who supervised the taking of
☐   each inventory, and the dollar amount and basis of each inventory.

DATE OF   DOLLAR AMOUNT OF INVENTORY
INVENTORY   INVENTORY SUPERVISOR   (Specify cost, market or other basis)

None   b. List the name and address of the person having possession of the records of each of the two inventories reported in a.,
☐   above.

DATE OF   NAME AND ADDRESSES OF CUSTODIAN
INVENTORY   OF INVENTORY RECORDS

19. Current partners, officers, directors and shareholders

None   a. If the debtor is a partnership, list the nature and percentage of partnership interest of each member of the partnership.
☐

                                                 PERCENTAGE
NAME AND ADDRESS   NATURE OF INTEREST   OF INTEREST

None b. If the debtor is a corporation, list all officers and directors of the corporation, and each stockholder who directly or
☐ indirectly owns, controls, or holds 5 percent or more of the voting securities of the corporation.

| | | NATURE AND PERCENTAGE |
NAME AND ADDRESS	TITLE	OF STOCK OWNERSHIP

---

20. Former partners, officers, directors and shareholders

None a. If the debtor is a partnership, list each member who withdrew from the partnership within one year immediately
☐ preceding the commencement of this case.

| | | DATE OF |
NAME	ADDRESS	WITHDRAWAL

None b. If the debtor is a corporation, list all officers, or directors whose relationship with the corporation terminated within one
☐ year immediately preceding the commencement of this case.

| | | DATE OF |
NAME AND ADDRESS	TITLE	TERMINATION

---

21. Withdrawals from a partnership or distributions by a corporation

None   If the debtor is a partnership or corporation, list all withdrawals or distributions credited or given to an insider,
☐ including compensation in any form, bonuses, loans, stock redemptions, options exercised and any other perquisite
during one year immediately preceding the commencement of this case.

| NAME AND ADDRESS | | AMOUNT OF MONEY |
| OF RECIPIENT, | DATE AND PURPOSE | OR DESCRIPTION |
RELATIONSHIP TO DEBTOR	OF WITHDRAWAL	AND VALUE OF PROPERTY

DECLARATION CONCERNING STATEMENT OF FINANCIAL AFFAIRS

DECLARATION UNDER PENALTY OF PERJURY BY INDIVIDUAL DEBTOR AND SPOUSE

I(We), _____ , declare under
penalty of perjury that I(we) have read the answers contained in the foregoing Statement of Financial Affairs and any attachments
thereto, and that they are true and correct.

Date _____   Signature _____
                                                                  Debtor

Date _____   Signature _____
                                                              (Joint Debtor, if any)

                                                    (If joint case, both spouses must sign)

....

DECLARATION UNDER PENALTY OF PERJURY ON BEHALF OF CORPORATION OR PARTNERSHIP

(Corporation) I, _____ , the _____
of the Corporation named as debtor in this case, declare under penalty of perjury that I have read the answers contained in the
foregoing Statement of Financial Affairs and any attachments thereto, and that they are true and correct.

(Partnership) I, _____ , *(check one)*
□ a member   (□ an authorized agent) of the Partnership named as debtor in this case, declare under penalty of perjury that I have
read the answers contained in the foregoing Statement of Financial Affairs and any attachments thereto, and that they are true and
correct.

Date _____   Signature _____

                                                         _____
                                                         (Print or type name of individual signing on behalf of debtor)

                                                         Title _____

(An individual signing on behalf of a partnership or corporation must indicate position or relationship to debtor.)

....

Penalty for making a false statement or concealing property: Fine of up to $500,000 or imprisonment for up to 5 years or both.
18 U.S.C. §§ 152 and 3571.

MASTER MAILING LIST

Debtor(s) _____

UNITED STATES BANKRUPTCY COURT

_____ District of _____

Case No. _____

(PLEASE READ REVERSE SIDE BEFORE COMPLETING)

Page _____ of _____ Page(s)

In re _____   Case No. _____
                                                                    (If known)
_____ , Debtor(s)

SCHEDULE A - REAL PROPERTY

Except as directed below, list all real property in which the debtor has any legal, equitable, or future interest, including all property owned as a co-tenant, community property, or in which the debtor has a life estate. Include any property in which the debtor holds rights and powers exercisable for the debtor's own benefit. If the debtor is married, state whether husband, wife, or both own the property by placing an "H," "W," "J," or "C" in the column labeled "Husband, Wife, Joint or Community." If the debtor holds no interest in real property, write "None" under "Description and Location of Property."

Do not include interests in executory contracts and unexpired leases on this schedule. List them in Schedule G - Executory Contracts and Unexpired Leases.

If an entity claims to have a lien or hold a secured interest in any property, state the amount of the secured claim. See Schedule D. If no entity claims to hold a secured interest in the property, write "None" in the column labeled "Amount of Secured Claim."

If the debtor is an individual or if a joint petition is filed, state the amount of any exemption claimed in the property only in Schedule C - Property Claimed as Exempt.

DESCRIPTION AND LOCATION OF PROPERTY	NATURE OF DEBTOR'S INTEREST IN PROPERTY	HUSBAND, WIFE, JOINT OR COMMUNITY	CURRENT MARKET VALUE OF DEBTOR'S INTEREST IN PROPERTY WITHOUT DEDUCTING ANY SECURED CLAIM OR EXEMPTION	AMOUNT OF SECURED CLAIM
		Total	$	

(Report also on Summary of Schedules.)

In re _____   Case No. _____
                                                                              (If known)
_____ , Debtor(s)

SCHEDULE B - PERSONAL PROPERTY

Except as directed below, list all personal property of the debtor of whatever kind. If the debtor has no property in one or more of the categories, place an "X" in the appropriate position in the column labeled "None." If additional space is needed in any category, attach a separate sheet properly identified with the case name, case number, and the number of the category. If the debtor is married, state whether husband, wife, or both own the property by placing an "H," "W," "J," or "C" in the column labeled "Husband, Wife, Joint, or Community." If the debtor is an individual or a joint petition is filed, state the amount of any exemptions claimed only in Schedule C - Property Claimed as Exempt.

Do not list interests in executory contracts and unexpired leases on this schedule. List them in Schedule G - Executory Contracts and Unexpired Leases.

If the property is being held for the debtor by someone else, state that person's name and address under "Description and Location of Property."

TYPE OF PROPERTY	NONE	DESCRIPTION AND LOCATION OF PROPERTY	HUSBAND, WIFE, JOINT OR COMMUNITY	CURRENT MARKET VALUE OF DEBTOR'S INTEREST IN PROPERTY, WITH-OUT DEDUCTING ANY SECURED CLAIM OR EXEMPTION
1. Cash on hand				
2. Checking, savings or other financial accounts, certificates of deposit, or shares in banks, savings and loan, thrift, building and loan, and homestead associations, or credit unions, brokerage houses, or cooperatives.				
3. Security deposits with public utilities, telephone companies, landlords, and others.				
4. Household goods and furnishings, including audio, video, and computer equipment.				
5. Books, pictures and other art objects, antiques, stamp, coin, record, compact disc, and other collections or collectibles.				
6. Wearing apparel.				
7. Furs and jewelry.				
8. Firearms and sports, photographic, and other hobby equipment.				
9. Interests in insurance policies. Name insurance company of each policy and itemize surrender or refund value of each.				
10. Annuities. Itemize and name each issuer.				

In re _____   Case No. _____
                                                                    (If known)
_____ , Debtor(s)

SCHEDULE C - PROPERTY CLAIMED AS EXEMPT

Debtor elects the exemption to which debtor is entitled under

(Check one box)

☐ 11 U.S.C. § 522(b)(1)   Exemptions provided in 11 U.S.C. § 522(d). Note: These exemptions are available only in certain states.

☐ 11 U.S.C. § 522(b)(2)   Exemptions available under applicable nonbankruptcy federal laws, state or local law where the debtor's domicile has been located for the 180 days immediately preceding the filing of the petition, or for a longer portion of the 180-day period than in any other place, and the debtor's interest as a tenant by the entirety or joint tenant to the extent the interest is exempt from process under applicable nonbankruptcy law.

DESCRIPTION OF PROPERTY	SPECIFY LAW PROVIDING EACH EXEMPTION	VALUE OF CLAIMED EXEMPTION	CURRENT MARKET VALUE OF PROPERTY WITHOUT DEDUCTING EXEMPTIONS

In re _____   Case No. _____

_____ , Debtor(s)   (If known)

SCHEDULE D - CREDITORS HOLDING SECURED CLAIMS

State the name, mailing address, including zip code, and account number, if any, of all entities holding claims secured by property of the debtor as of the date of filing of the petition. List creditors holding all types of secured interests such as judgment liens, garnishments, statutory liens, mortgages, deeds of trust, and other security interests. List creditors in alphabetical order to the extent practicable. If all secured creditors will not fit on this page, use the continuation sheet provided.

If any entity other than a spouse in a joint case may be jointly liable on a claim, place an "X" in the column labeled "Codebtor," include the entity on the appropriate schedule of creditors, and complete Schedule H - Codebtors. If a joint petition is filed, state whether husband, wife, both of them, or the marital community may be liable on each claim by placing an "H," "W," "J," or "C" in the column labeled "Husband, Wife, Joint, or Community."

If the claim is contingent, place an "X" in the column labeled "Contingent." If the claim is unliquidated, place an "X" in the column labeled "Unliquidated." If the claim is disputed, place an "X" in the column labeled "Disputed." (You may need to place an "X" in more than one of these three columns.)

Report the total of all claims listed on this schedule in the box labeled "Total" on the last sheet of the completed schedule. Report this total also on the Summary of Schedules.

☐ Check this box if debtor has no creditors holding secured claims to report on this Schedule D.

CREDITOR'S NAME AND MAILING ADDRESS INCLUDING ZIP CODE	CODEBTOR	HUSBAND, WIFE, JOINT, OR COMMUNITY	DATE CLAIM WAS INCURRED, NATURE OF LIEN, AND DESCRIPTION AND MARKET VALUE OF PROPERTY SUBJECT TO LIEN	CONTINGENT	UNLIQUIDATED	DISPUTED	AMOUNT OF CLAIM WITHOUT DEDUCTING VALUE OF COLLATERAL	UNSECURED PORTION, IF ANY
ACCOUNT NO.								
			VALUE $					
ACCOUNT NO.								
			VALUE $					
ACCOUNT NO.								
			VALUE $					
ACCOUNT NO.								
			VALUE $					

_____ Continuation sheets attached

Subtotal (Total of this page) $ _____

Total (Use only on last page) $ _____

(Report total also on Summary of Schedules)

© 1991. ALPHA PUBLICATIONS OF AMERICA, INC — P.O. BOX 13881 — TUCSON, ARIZONA 85732-3881   FORM ABK-7007

In re _____

_____ , Debtor(s)

Case No. _____

(If known)

SCHEDULE E - CREDITORS HOLDING UNSECURED PRIORITY CLAIMS

A complete list of claims entitled to priority, listed separately by type of priority, is to be set forth on the sheets provided. Only holders of unsecured claims entitled to priority should be listed in this schedule. In the boxes provided on the attached sheets, state the name and mailing address, including zip code, and account number if any, of all entities holding priority claims against the debtor or the property of the debtor, as of the date of the filing of this petition.

If any entity other than a spouse in a joint case may be jointly liable on a claim, place an "X" in the column labeled "Codebtor," include the entity on the appropriate schedule of creditors, and complete Schedule H - Codebtors. If a joint petition is filed, state whether husband, wife, both of them, or the marital community may be liable on each claim by placing an "H," "W," "J," or "C" in the column labeled "Husband, Wife, Joint, or Community."

If the claim is contingent, place an "X" in the column labeled "Contingent." If the claim is unliquidated, place an "X" in the column labeled 'Unliquidated." If the claim is disputed, place an "X" in the column labeled "Disputed." (You may need to place an "X" in more than one of these three columns.)

Report the total of claims listed on each sheet in the box labeled, "Subtotal" on each sheet. Report the total of all claims listed on this Schedule E in the box labeled "Total" on the last sheet of the completed schedule. Repeat this total also on the Summary of Schedules.

☐ Check this box if debtor has no creditors holding unsecured priority claims to report on this Schedule E.

TYPES OF PRIORITY CLAIMS

☐ **Extensions of credit in an involuntary case**

Claims arising in the ordinary course of the debtor's business or financial affairs after the commencement of the case but before the earlier of the appointment of a trustee or the order for relief. 11 U.S.C. § 507(a)(2).

☐ **Wages, salaries, and commissions**

Wages, salaries, and commissions, including vacation, severance, and sick leave pay owing to employees, up to a maximum of $2000 per employee, earned within 90 days immediately preceding the filing of the original petition, or the cessation of business, whichever occurred first, to the extent provided in 11 U.S.C. § 507(a)(3).

☐ **Contributions to employee benefit plans**

Money owed to employee benefit plans for services rendered within 180 days immediately preceding the filing of the original petition, or the cessation of business, whichever occurred first, to the extent provided in 11 U.S.C. § 507(a)(4).

☐ **Certain farmers and fishermen**

Claims of certain farmers and fishermen, up to a maximum of $2000 per farmer or fisherman, against the debtor, as provided in 11 U.S.C. § 507(a)(5).

☐ **Deposits by individuals**

Claims of individuals up to a maximum of $900 for deposits for the purchase, lease, or rental of property or services for personal family, or household use, that were not delivered or provided. 11 U.S.C. § 507(a)(6).

☐ **Taxes and other certain debts owed to governmental units**

Taxes, customs duties, and penalties owing to federal, state, and local governmental units as set forth in 11 U.S.C. § 507(a)(7).

_____ continuation sheets attached

In re _____ Case No. _____
                                              (If known)
_____ , Debtor(s)

SCHEDULE F - CREDITORS HOLDING UNSECURED NONPRIORITY CLAIMS

State the name, mailing address, including zip code, and account number, if any, of all entities holding UNSECURED claims without priority against the debtor or the property of the debtor, as of the date of filing of the petition. Do not include claims listed in Schedules D and E. If all creditors will not fit on this page, use the continuation sheet provided.

If any entity other than a spouse in a joint case may be jointly liable on a claim, place an "X" in the column labeled "Codebtor," include the entity on the appropriate schedule of creditors, and complete Schedule H - Codebtors. If a joint petition is filed, state whether husband, wife, both of them, or the marital community may be liable on each claim by placing an "H," "W," "J," or "C" in the column labeled "Husband, Wife, Joint, or Community."

If the claim is contingent, place an "X" in the column labeled "Contingent." If the claim is unliquidated, place an "X" in the column labeled "Unliquidated." If the claim is disputed, place an "X" in the column labeled "Disputed." (You may need to place an "X" in more than one of these three columns.)

Report the total of all claims listed on this schedule in the box labeled "Total" on the last sheet of the completed schedule. Report this total also on the Summary of Schedules.

☐ Check this box if debtor has no creditors holding unsecured nonpriority claims to report on this Schedule F.

CREDITOR'S NAME AND MAILING ADDRESS INCLUDING ZIP CODE	CODEBTOR	HUSBAND, WIFE, JOINT OR COMMUNITY	DATE CLAIM WAS INCURRED, AND CONSIDERATION FOR CLAIM, IF CLAIM IS SUBJECT TO SETOFF, SO STATE	CONTINGENT	UNLIQUIDATED	DISPUTED	AMOUNT OF CLAIM
ACCOUNT NO.							
ACCOUNT NO.							
ACCOUNT NO.							
ACCOUNT NO.							
			Subtotal (Total of this page)				$
_____ Continuation sheets attached			Total (Use only on last page of completed Schedule F)				$

(Report total also on Summary of Schedules)

© 1991 ALPHA PUBLICATIONS OF AMERICA, INC — P.O. BOX 13881 — TUCSON, ARIZONA 85732-3881   FORM ABK-7011

In re _____   Case No. _____
                                                            (If known)
_____ , Debtor(s)

SCHEDULE G - EXECUTORY CONTRACTS AND UNEXPIRED LEASES

Describe all executory contracts of any nature and all unexpired leases of real or personal property. Include any timeshare interests.

State nature of debtor's interest in contract, i.e., "Purchaser," "Agent," etc. State whether debtor is the lessor or lessee of a lease.

Provide the names and complete mailing addresses of all other parties to each lease or contract described.

NOTE: A party listed on this schedule will not receive notice of the filing of this case unless the party is also scheduled in the appropriate schedule of creditors.

☐ Check this box if debtor has no executory contracts or unexpired leases.

NAME AND MAILING ADDRESS, INCLUDING ZIP CODE, OF OTHER PARTIES TO LEASE OR CONTRACT	DESCRIPTION OF CONTRACT OR LEASE AND NATURE OF DEBTOR'S INTEREST. STATE WHETHER LEASE IS FOR NONRESIDENTIAL REAL PROPERTY. STATE CONTRACT NUMBER OF ANY GOVERNMENT CONTRACT

© 1991 ALPHA PUBLICATIONS OF AMERICA, INC. — P.O. BOX 13881   TUCSON, ARIZONA 85732-3881   FORM ABK-7015

In re _____   Case No. _____
                                                          (If known)
_____ , Debtor(s)

SCHEDULE H - CODEBTORS

Provide the information requested concerning any person or entity, other than a spouse in a joint case that is also liable on any debts listed by debtor in the schedules of creditors. Include all guarantors and co-signers. In community property states, a married debtor not filing a joint case should report the name and address of the nondebtor spouse on this schedule. Include all names used by the nondebtor spouse during the six years immediately preceding the commencement of this case.

☐ Check this box if debtor has no codebtors.

NAME AND ADDRESS OF CODEBTOR	NAME AND ADDRESS OF CREDITOR

In re _____ Case No. _____
                                                    (If known)
_____ , Debtor(s)

SCHEDULE I - CURRENT INCOME OF INDIVIDUAL DEBTOR(S)

The column labeled "Spouse" must be completed in all cases filed by joint debtors and by a married debtor in a Chapter 12 or 13 case whether or not a joint petition is filed, unless the spouses are separated and a joint petition is not filed.

Debtor's Marital Status	DEPENDENTS OF DEBTOR AND SPOUSE		
	NAMES	AGE	RELATIONSHIP

EMPLOYMENT:	DEBTOR	SPOUSE
Occupation Name of Employer		
How long employed		
Address of Employer		

Income (Estimate of average monthly income):	DEBTOR	SPOUSE
Current monthly gross wages, salary, and commissions (pro rate if not paid monthly)	$ _____	$ _____
Estimated monthly overtime	$ _____	$ _____
SUBTOTAL	$ _____	$ _____
LESS PAYROLL DEDUCTIONS		
a. Payroll taxes and social security	$ _____	$ _____
b. Insurance	$ _____	$ _____
c. Union dues	$ _____	$ _____
d. Other (Specify) _____	$ _____	$ _____
SUBTOTAL OF PAYROLL DEDUCTIONS	$ _____	$ _____
TOTAL NET MONTHLY TAKE HOME PAY	$ _____	$ _____
Regular income from operation of business or profession or farm (attach detailed statement)	$ _____	$ _____
Income from real property	$ _____	$ _____
Interest and dividends	$ _____	$ _____
Alimony, maintenance or support payments payable to the debtor for the debtor's use or that of dependents listed above	$ _____	$ _____
Social security or other government assistance (Specify) _____	$ _____	$ _____
Pension or retirement income	$ _____	$ _____
Other monthly income (Specify) _____	$ _____	$ _____
_____	$ _____	$ _____
_____	$ _____	$ _____
TOTAL MONTHLY INCOME	$ _____	$ _____

TOTAL COMBINED MONTHLY INCOME $ _____   (Report also on Summary of Schedules)

Describe any increase or decrease of more than 10% in any of the above categories anticipated to occur within the year following the filing of this document.

· 1991 ALPHA PUBLICATIONS OF AMERICA INC — P.O. BOX 13881 · TUCSON ARIZONA 85732-3881   FORM ABK-7017

In re _____   Case No. _____
_____ , Debtor(s)   (If known)

SCHEDULE J - CURRENT EXPENDITURES OF INDIVIDUAL DEBTORS

Complete this schedule by estimating the average monthly expenses of the debtor and the debtor's family. Pro rate any payments made bi-weekly, quarterly, semi-annually, or annually to show monthly rate.

☐ Check this box if a joint petition is filed and debtor's spouse maintains a separate household. Complete a separate schedule of expenditures labeled "Spouse."

Rent or home mortgage payment (include lot rented for mobile home)	$ _____
Are real estate taxes included? Yes _____ No _____	
Is property insurance included? Yes _____ No _____	
Utilities: Electricity and heating fuel	$ _____
Water and sewer	$ _____
Telephone	$ _____
Other _____	$ _____
Home Maintenance (Repairs and upkeep)	$ _____
Food	$ _____
Clothing	$ _____
Laundry and dry cleaning	$ _____
Medical and dental expenses	$ _____
Transportation (not including car payments)	$ _____
Recreation, clubs and entertainment, newspapers, magazines, etc.	$ _____
Charitable contributions	$ _____
Insurance (not deducted from wages or included in home mortgage payments)	
Homeowner's or renter's	$ _____
Life	$ _____
Health	$ _____
Auto	$ _____
Other _____	$ _____
Taxes (not deducted from wages or included in home mortgage payments)	
(Specify) _____	$ _____
Installment payments (In chapter 12 and 13 cases, do not list payments to be included in the plan)	
Auto	$ _____
Other _____	$ _____
Other _____	$ _____
Alimony, maintenance, and support paid to others	$ _____
Payments for support of additional dependents not living at your home	$ _____
Regular expenses from operation of business, profession, or farm (attach detailed statement)	$ _____
Other _____	$ _____
TOTAL MONTHLY EXPENSES (Report also on Summary of Schedules)	$ _____

(FOR CHAPTER 12 DEBTORS ONLY)

Provide the information requested below, including whether plan payments are to be made bi-weekly, monthly, annually, or at some other regular interval.

A. Total projected monthly income	$ _____
B. Total projected monthly expenses	$ _____
C. Excess income (A minus B)	$ _____
D. Total amount to be paid into plan each _____	$ _____
(interval)	

In re _____   Case No. _____
                                                                    (If known)
_____ , Debtor(s)

SUMMARY OF SCHEDULES

Indicate as to each schedule whether that schedule is attached and state the number of pages in each. Report the totals from Schedules A, B, C, D, E, F, I, and J in the boxes provided. Add the amounts from Schedules A and B to determine the total amount of the debtor's assets. Add the amounts from Schedules D, E, and F to determine the total amount of the debtor's liabilities.

NAME OF SCHEDULE	ATTACHED (YES/NO)	NO. OF SHEETS	AMOUNTS SCHEDULED		
			ASSETS	LIABILITIES	OTHER
A - Real Property			$		
B - Personal Property			$		
C - Property Claimed As Exempt					
D - Creditors Holding Secured Claims				$	
E - Creditors Holding Unsecured Priority Claims				$	
F - Creditors Holding Unsecured Nonpriority Claims				$.	
G - Executory Contracts and Unexpired Leases					
H - Codebtors					
I - Current Income of Individual Debtor(s)					$
J - Current Expenditures of Individual Debtor(s)					$
Total Number of Sheets in ALL Schedules					
Total Assets	$				
Total Liabilities	$				

© 1991, ALPHA PUBLICATIONS OF AMERICA, INC. — P.O. BOX 13881 — TUCSON, ARIZONA 85732-3881   FORM ABK-7001

In re _____ Case No. _____
_____ , Debtor(s) (If known)

DECLARATION CONCERNING DEBTOR'S SCHEDULES

DECLARATION UNDER PENALTY OF PERJURY BY INDIVIDUAL DEBTOR AND SPOUSE

I(We), _____ , declare under
penalty of perjury that I(we) have read the foregoing Summary and Schedules, consisting of _____
(Total on Summary Page plus 1)
sheets, and that they are true and correct to the best of my(our) knowledge, information and belief.

Date _____ Signature _____
Debtor

Date _____ Signature _____
(Joint Debtor, if any)
(If joint case, both spouses must sign)

....

DECLARATION UNDER PENALTY OF PERJURY ON BEHALF OF CORPORATION OR PARTNERSHIP

(Corporation) I, _____ , the _____
of the Corporation named as debtor in this case, declare under penalty of perjury that I have read the foregoing Summary and
Schedules, consisting of _____ sheets, and that they are true and correct to the best of my knowledge,
(Total on Summary Page plus 1)
information, and belief.

(Partnership) I, _____ , *(check one)*
☐ a member (☐ an authorized agent) of the Partnership named as debtor in this case, declare under penalty of perjury that I have
read the foregoing Summary and Schedules, consisting of _____ sheets, and that they are true and
(Total on Summary Page plus 1)
correct to the best of my knowledge, information and belief.

Date _____ Signature _____

_____
(Print or type name of individual signing on behalf of debtor)

Title _____

(An individual signing on behalf of a partnership or corporation must indicate position or relationship to debtor.)

....

Penalty for making a false statement or concealing property: Fine of up to $500,000 or imprisonment for up to 5 years or both.
18 U.S.C. §§ 152 and 3571.

● 1991, ALPHA PUBLICATIONS OF AMERICA, INC. — P.O. BOX 13881 — TUCSON, ARIZONA 85732-3881   FORM ABK-7019

Name

Address

City/State/Zip Code

Phone No. _____

☐ Debtor(s) in pro per
☐ Attorney for debtor

UNITED STATES BANKRUPTCY COURT

_____ DISTRICT OF _____

In re

)
)
)
)

CASE NO. _____

CHAPTER _____

**INFORMATION REGARDING
PRIOR BANKRUPTCY PROCEEDING**

Debtor(s).

1. A petition under the Bankruptcy Act of 1898 or the Bankruptcy Reform Act of 1978 has previously been filed by or against the debtor, his/her spouse, an affiliate of the debtor, any copartnership or joint venture of which debtor is or formerly was a general or limited partner, or a member, or any corporation of which the debtor is a director, officer, or person in control, as follows: (Set forth the complete number and title of such a prior proceeding, date filed, nature thereof, the Bankruptcy Judge and Court to whom assigned, whether still pending and, if not, the disposition thereof. If none, so indicate.)

2. A petition under the Bankruptcy Reform Act, including amendments thereof, has been filed by or against the debtor/joint debtor within the last 180 days: (Set forth the complete number and title of such prior proceeding, date filed, nature of proceeding, the Bankruptcy Judge and Court whom assigned, whether still pending, and if not, the disposition thereof. If none, so indicate.)

Execution date: _____

_____
Debtor

_____
Joint Debtor

UNSWORN DECLARATION UNDER PENALTY OF PERJURY

I declare, under penalty of perjury, that the foregoing is true and correct.

Executed on _____

_____
Debtor

_____
Joint Debtor

Index

telephone bills, 14
utility bills, 22-23
on credit cards, 21-22
Refinancing your mortgage,
13-14
Relocation, 12
Retirement plans, 31-32

Telecommunications Research
& Action Center, 15
Telephone bills, 14
Tightwad Gazette, 26
Trustee, 71-72
Trusts, 30-32
TRW, 41ff

S

Sam's Club, 16
Saving, 12ff
Sczapluski, Vincent, 14
Smart Sense, 18
Stay lift motions, 73-74

U

Utility bills, 22-23

V

Voluntary bankruptcy, 48ff

T

Taylor, Barbara, 18